The House That Cleans Itself

Mindy Starns Clark

HARVEST HOUSE PUBLISHERS
EUGENE, OREGON

JUN 0 3 2014

To protect the privacy of individuals who completed the author's housekeeping surveys and/or shared their stories, names have been changed throughout this book.

Some graphics inside this book were created by Linda Moye, with additional graphics by Amy Starns. Used by permission.

Cover by Dugan Design Group, Bloomington, Minnesota

Cover illustration © Michael Lotenero / Photodisc Green / Getty Images

THE HOUSE THAT CLEANS ITSELF
Copyright © 2007, 2013 by Mindy Starns Clark
Published by Harvest House Publishers
Eugene, Oregon 97402
www.harvesthousepublishers.com

ISBN 978-0-7369-4987-3 (pbk.)
ISBN 978-0-7369-4988-0 (eBook)

The Library of Congress has cataloged the edition as follows:

Library of Congress Cataloging-in-Publication Data
    Clark, Mindy Starns.
    The house that cleans itself / Mindy Starns Clark.
       p. cm.
    ISBN 978-0-7369-1880-0 (pbk.)
    1. House cleaning. 2. Christian life. I. Title
    TX324.C576 2007
    648'.5—dc22

Printed in the United States of America

13 14 15 16 17 18 19 20 21 / BP-CD / 10 9 8 7 6 5 4 3 2 1

Dedicated with much love to my dear friend
Kay Justus.
Thanks for putting up with me as a roommate all those years ago,
in college and beyond,
when housekeeping was a vague intention,
the vacuum cleaner mostly served as a coatrack,
and the oven was for hiding dirty dishes.

That was then, this is now...

Acknowledgments

Many thanks to

> My husband, John, for loving me so completely, even in the midst of mess. You are my helpmate, soul mate, and best friend.

> My daughters, Emily and Lauren, the most supportive kids a mom could ever ask for.

> Kim Moore, my beloved editor and dear friend; Barbara Gordon; and all of the amazing folks at Harvest House Publishers.

> Helen Lerner, MD, for invaluable insight into the psychological aspects of housekeeping issues.

Thanks also to

> "Dr. Gadget" Dave Dettman, Helen Styer Hannigan, Hannah Keeley, Elisa Marshall, Linda Moye, Amy Starns, Jackie Starns, Vanessa Thompson, Shari Weber, Joy Williams and the "Memphis HTCI Sistas," and the ever-helpful members of CONSENSUS and ChiLibris.

+   +   +   +   +

I am deeply indebted to those who were willing to share their deepest messy-house secrets, fears, questions, problems, feelings, and challenges during the process of writing and later updating *The House That Cleans Itself*. To protect the privacy of these generous people and their families, I have changed most of the names used throughout this book. Thus, to all of my anonymous helpers, you know who you are, and my hope is you will see how your own transparency has helped so many others who face the same struggles. Thank you!

Finally, my heartfelt gratitude goes out to everyone who has given this system a chance since it first came out and then took the time to provide feedback through e-mails, reviews, blogs, comments, letters, and more. Your input has had a tremendous impact on the new and improved version of this book. You have blessed and encouraged me more than you can imagine!

Contents

Part 4: Supplemental Content

Part 1

Stop and Consider

By wisdom a house is built,
and through understanding
it is established;
through knowledge its rooms are
filled with rare and beautiful
treasures.

Proverbs 24:3-4

What to Expect from This Book

The House That Cleans Itself is a how-to guide that reveals, step-by-step, a unique and creative system that will:

+ take a house that *tends to be messy* and turn it into a house that *tends to be neat*

+ take a cleaning routine that takes up *far too much time* and turn it into a cleaning routine that is *shockingly fast*

+ turn family members' *mess-inducing behaviors* into *naturally tidy behaviors,* often without them even realizing it

+ take a life where *the minutes are eaten away* by ordinary household tasks and turn it into a life with *time to spare* for things that really count

+ take a person who *feels like a failure* in caring for his or her home and change that person into someone who is *unburdened, unashamed, and successful* in caring for the home

As you can see, the House That Cleans Itself System is designed to make your home easier to keep clean, easier to manage, and easier to enjoy than ever before.

1

A Better Way

Let the redeemed of the LORD tell their story...
Let them give thanks to the LORD for his unfailing love
and his wonderful deeds for mankind.

PSALM 107:2,8

To say I've struggled with housekeeping my whole life would be an understatement. As a child I had to carve paths through my toys just to get into bed at night. Later, as a young woman on my own, I was still carving paths, ones that wound throughout my apartment. It's not that I liked living that way, but I just couldn't seem to get a handle on all of my stuff, even as an adult.

In my late twenties, once I was engaged to be married, I decided it was time to get my act together. I naively assumed the mere resolve to change was all it would take. With enough willpower and determination I really would be able to keep a neat and orderly home for the first time in my life.

Oh, boy. Was I in for a surprise.

Let's just say that once I was married and settled into my first home, I really did try. I tried as hard as I could, in fact, and of course my sweet husband pitched in as he was able. But with law school each day and work each night, he was juggling more than I was, so the bulk of the cleaning fell to me. It didn't take long to see that the battle, once again, was going to be lost. Somehow I managed to keep things from getting to the path-carving level, but keeping our home clean remained a daily struggle between the mess and me. As it turned out, willpower and determination were no match for my innate tendency toward clutter and chaos.

Adding two children into the mix over the next few years only made a bad situation worse. I loved being a wife and mother, and I wanted our home to be a place of peace and rest, not disarray and disorder. But when it came to housekeeping, the children's added mess turned out to be the straw that broke the camel's back, especially because I was also working a part-time job and trying to become a writer on the side. With no spare time, no energy, and no cleaning skills, I would have raised a white flag if I could, but staying home with the kids meant forgoing certain luxuries such as maids or cleaning services. Besides, despite my past failures and my limited homemaking skills, I persisted in the notion that I could do better if only I tried harder.

So I tried harder.

Yet chaos and disorder continued to reign. Oh, there were a few successes along the way—the occasional spring cleaning that was actually finished before the following winter, the rare party or gathering where we didn't have to lock half the doors for fear our guests might see the messes behind them—and these small victories offered us glimpses of hope amidst the failure. But there were still more failures than successes.

Time Marches On

Fortunately, homemaking became somewhat easier as the kids grew older and started school, but I never did get a handle on how to keep a house consistently clean and organized. The truth was, no matter how hard I tried, the place was messy far more often than it was neat. We were always losing things, stepping on things, or having to buy new things because we couldn't find the things we already had.

At least I was finding success in other areas. Chief among them was when my lifelong dream came true and I sold my first novel to a publisher. They wanted an entire series, in fact, so practically overnight I went from being an at-home mom with a little part-time job and a big dream to an at-home mom working 50 to 60 hours per week at that dream as a professional author. If things had been messy before, my wonderful new career turned our world into an even bigger nightmare of disorganization, clutter, sticky cabinets, and laundry mountains.

We managed to muddle through for a few years until I was contracted for even more books. When we saw that my schedule wasn't going to clear up any time soon, we knew the time had come, at long last, to get a housekeeper. Finally, relief was in sight! Rescue was here! After years of struggle, our troubles were over...or so I assumed.

With visions of my own House Beautiful dancing in my head, I promptly hired an expert to come clean for me once a week. (Of course, that meant clearing mountains of stuff out of the way every time before she got there, but it was worth it.) She was indeed a veritable tornado of clean and never failed to make our home shiny and sparkly and smelling of lemons and freshness. Once she was gone, the place always looked beautiful.

After just a few hours, however, it would begin to fall apart again. By the next day, I would look around and find it hard to believe that a housekeeper had ever been there. Week after week after week, our home would become a disaster—*within 24 hours of having been cleaned!*— almost as if the stuff I'd put away before she came simply waited in hiding until she was gone to explode back out again.

I consoled myself that thanks to her efforts, at least there wasn't much dirt under all that clutter, but that thought was little comfort when faced with the chaos that stretched from one end of our home to the other, despite having weekly help.

What were we doing wrong?

Why couldn't we keep our house neat?

Housekeeping-wise, I felt as though I'd hit rock bottom. Tormented by what I saw as my ultimate failure as a woman, wife, and mother, I kept wondering what was the matter with me, where I'd gone wrong.

Why was this thing that seemed so easy for other people so difficult for us? For me?

Believe it or not, the answers to those questions—indeed, the solutions to my entire, lifelong housekeeping problem—were already beginning to fall into place, right under my own nose. I just hadn't realized it yet.

I Saw the Light

The change began with my sixth book. First in a new mystery series, *The Trouble with Tulip* features the adventures of Jo Tulip, a household hints expert who uses her unique knowledge of cleaning to solve crime. Despite my own messy world, I'd always had a strange fascination with household hints, and I thought this would be a clever and story-rich setup for a resourceful sleuth.

That series was great fun to write but also a real challenge because I wanted to derive key plot elements from my heroine's line of work. Doing the research required me to read numerous books on cleaning and organization, trolling for ideas on clever plot twists that could come from actual tricks and techniques of housekeeping. By the time I was halfway through researching the second novel in the series, *Blind Dates Can Be Murder,* I had read more than 40 books on housekeeping. In a sense, all that reading turned me into a veritable expert on everything from stain removal to household filing systems. Yet my own home was still as messy as ever.

As I continued to write adventures for my housecleaning-savvy heroine, I kept thinking about the irony of that. How could so much head knowledge *not* translate into the reality of a clean home for me? Ruminating on that paradox, I suddenly had an epiphany, followed by even more epiphanies, some of them quite shocking. Like a series of mental dynamite, it was as if a steel door blew open in my mind and the answers I'd been seeking my entire life revealed themselves at last. Finally, I understood truths that had eluded me all those years.

With these truths in hand, I began to figure out how someone like me—someone really, really bad at housekeeping—could get a house clean and keep it that way regardless of his or her own shortcomings.

At first it was just a theory, one I quietly tested in my home in a few small ways. When those attempts proved successful, I expanded this approach throughout my house and could see by the proof of victory that I was onto something big. For the first time in my life, my house was *staying* clean and organized—without much effort from me. Ecstatic, I foisted my plan on a few messier-than-average friends, who were astounded to find my ideas worked in their homes too.

After that I took things online. I asked questions, took polls, formed Internet groups. Word spread. More houses got clean and stayed that way. More people who had always thought of themselves as housekeeping failures slowly became housekeeping successes. Their homes were staying clean. We were all overjoyed.

Somehow, by the grace of God, I knew I had come up with a brand-new method for getting a house clean and keeping it that way, a method I had not run across *in more than 40 books on housekeeping*. Best of all, my unconventional new method worked for people who struggled in this area, perhaps for their entire lives. Naturally messy or naturally neat, it didn't matter. My plan simply worked. Our house was clean. Our struggle was over at last.

Summoning my nerve, I decided to take my plan even bigger and write a book about it. Fortunately, my publisher loved the idea. The original version of *The House That Cleans Itself* came out in 2007, an unassuming little book with a nifty cover and a catchy title and the most unlikely of authors ever to pen a housekeeping guide.

The Little Book with a Big Impact

My first book signing for *The House That Cleans Itself* was in a mall, and I can still remember the people who passed by, spotted the poster featuring the book's title, and burst out laughing.

"A house that cleans itself? Yeah, right. I'll take one of those!"

Most of them were being sarcastic. Yet over the next year enough people gave my concepts a chance that the book quietly became a bestseller. It was a mainstay on racks in grocery aisles and general stores around the world. It was translated into other languages, used for Bible studies and book club selections, and wait-listed at libraries across the country. To my delight, devotees of the plan started popping up across the web, ordinary people who had discovered the book and decided to write blogs and track their progress online with commentary, descriptions, and plenty of before-and-after photos.

I found myself being interviewed for articles about cleaning and organization, quoted in magazines such as *Family Circle, Woman's Day*, and *Parents*. Can you imagine? Me, of all people? It was both surreal and deeply gratifying.

Even more gratifying were the letters and e-mails I received from readers—hundreds of readers who wanted to ask questions or let me know the plan was working for them or simply thank me for helping them get their homes in order after a lifetime of failure and guilt and shame. Most of those letters were thrilling, though some were also quite sad—marriages strained to the breaking point by battles over mess. Hoarders desperate for release from their bondage of stuff. Clutterers who battled depression and were terrified to get their hopes up yet again just because they had found a new plan that sounded good. Time after time, I could feel the anguish coming through their words. I recognized that anguish.

It was my anguish. It was all our anguish, all of us who had spent years burdened by this problem that finally had a solution. And to think it all started with one small series of mental epiphanies. In the next chapter, I'll tell you all about those epiphanies and how they led to this life-changing plan. I'll explain what a House That Cleans Itself is, how it works, and how you can make it work for you.

Whether you struggle with housekeeping or not, this book will be a real eye-opener for you. In fact, what you hold in your hand is probably unlike any other cleaning book you've ever seen. Unique as it is, I think you'll find that my ideas make sense—perhaps in a way no other cleaning advice ever has before. And that's the point, as you'll learn in the next chapter. If you struggle with cleaning, or even if you have a handle on cleaning but sometimes find yourself thinking, *There must be an easier way*, I'm here to tell you there is. You're holding it in your hand. So...

Are you ready to conquer your mess once and for all?

Do you want to get your home twice as neat in half the time?

Believe it or not, you *can* break free from the bondage of your own chaos and clutter, even after a lifetime of struggle. The system works for me. It's working for tens of thousands of others as well. Now it's your turn.

Keep reading to find out how you, too, can have a House That Cleans Itself.

My Most Embarrassing Messy House Story
—Why Else Would You Bother?—
BY MARLEE S.

One morning when I was feeling particularly energetic and ambitious, I smiled at my four-year-old daughter across the breakfast table and announced, "Today I'm going to clean this place, top to bottom."

"Yay!" she replied, eyes lit with excitement. "Who's coming over?"

2

The HTCI System

Hope deferred makes the heart sick,
but a longing fulfilled is a tree of life.

PROVERBS 13:12

Welcome to the House That Cleans Itself method of housekeeping, or the "HTCI System" for short. This book will show you how to conquer your mess once and for all, regardless of your past track record at keeping your home clean.

Make no mistake, this guide contains none of the conventional wisdom or standard rules of thumb that cleaning experts frequently espouse. It is, in fact, unlike any housekeeping how-to you've ever seen. At first glance it may seem weird and unconventional and perhaps even a bit startling, but it's designed for real people who live in real houses—and it really works.

This is not some standard-issue how-to manual about making your home as spotless and pristine as a museum. Instead, it is designed to help you attain a living, breathing, working home—one that allows for life but recovers quickly and easily from the messes that life inevitably brings.

By definition, then, a House That Cleans Itself is one where:

+ all rooms have the pleasing appearance of neatness

+ all surfaces are healthfully clean

+ the closets and drawers are well organized so they serve as fully functioning tools for daily living

+ the systems for accomplishing household tasks work smoothly for every member of the family

+ the odds and ends of life are easily processed, not frequently misplaced, and tend not to form clutter

+ all necessary and regular cleaning tasks take minimal time to accomplish

+ the primary feeling throughout the home is one of peace and order, not disarray and chaos

The goal of a House That Cleans Itself is not a *perfect* home. You may be surprised to learn that perfectionism actually makes your house worse, not better, something that will be addressed at length in a later chapter. No, the goal of a House That Cleans Itself is a *clean-enough* house. By tossing out perfectionist standards impossible to achieve, your home will actually be cleaner much more consistently than ever before.

So how clean is *clean enough*? I like to say that's where kids can be kids without leaving disaster behind when they are done, where Dad will do the "neat thing" rather than the "messy thing" without even being reminded, where Mom can sit on the couch and close her eyes once in a while—and not because she's exhausted by the mess but because she's relaxed by the clean. It's a house where you won't be embarrassed if friends drop by without warning, where items can be found without too much effort, where things are so organized that a sense of order begins to permeate into other areas of life as well.

Most importantly, a house is clean enough when all of the above is achieved in a way that at times feels almost effortless. Make no mistake, it takes some work up front to turn your home into a House That Cleans Itself. But once you do, maintaining that cleanliness will be easier than you've ever imagined. True to its name, a House That Cleans Itself is ultimately one that stays so consistently clean with so little effort that it almost feels as though the house is cleaning itself.

Who Needs It

Use this handy chart to decide if this book can help you.

If you:	Then you:
Struggle with housekeeping...	...need this book—it will change your life!
Do okay at housekeeping...	...will love this book. Its unconventional approach will help you look at the topic in a whole new way, helping you to refine your systems, reduce your cleaning time, and save effort and aggravation all over the house.
Have someone in your life who struggles with housekeeping...	...will find this book very useful. It will give you insight and understanding, and it will show you how best to help them, motivate them, and work with them in ways that will help them succeed where other plans have failed.
Are an amazing housekeeper...	...will find this book interesting—and you may pick up a few clever cleaning suggestions. Primarily, it will give you a whole new understanding of what life is like for those who have no natural talent for cleaning and are always struggling in this area.

At times, however, this book may also leave you scratching your head and going "Huh?" Because you're naturally gifted at housekeeping, much of the advice herein might sound strange to you indeed. But if you'd like to see the world of cleaning through other eyes, you won't be disappointed. May your heart grow with compassion and your mind with acceptance—even as you discover a new work-saving tip or two along the way!

The HTCI System will work for anyone, naturally messy or born neat, but it is especially effective for those who have always struggled in this area. Designed by a fellow struggler, this is the perfect plan for those who have never been able to get a handle on household mess before. It has worked for so many others. It works for me. It will work for you.

The Creation of the HTCI System

In the first chapter I explained that I read more than 40 books on housekeeping while doing research for a series of mystery novels. All that reading led to a startling series of epiphanies, which led to the creation of the HTCI System. Following is a description of those realizations and the radical new housekeeping method that rose out of them. I've chosen to lay things out this way not because I think you need to hear more of my own personal saga, but because I think this is the best approach for explaining what a House That Cleans Itself really is, how it works, and how you can make it work for you.

Realization 1—I Think Differently

The first thing that struck me after reading so many books about housekeeping was that every single one of them had been written by someone who was outstanding at keeping a home clean. These people were qualified, knowledgeable, and passionate on the topic. In other words, they were nothing like me at all.

They didn't think like me. They didn't act like me. They didn't live like me. Yet in each of their books, they were trying to advise me.

They were spouting what were to them "simple" cleaning plans and "clever" rules of thumb and "helpful" suggestions, none of which sounded simple, clever, or helpful to me in any way whatsoever.

In fact, I had found many of their ideas downright ludicrous. Even without trying out their suggestions, I had known they weren't going to work for me. The people who wrote these books couldn't help me with my cleaning problems because we didn't speak the same language. We weren't on the same wavelength.

Take, for example, their myriad rules of thumb about clearing clutter. Every time I read yet another adage about, "If you haven't used it in the past year (past six months, past whatever, past fill-in-the-blank), then get rid of it." I would think, *Are you crazy? This would make a perfect costume someday if my kid ever has to be a turtle. And I'm going to turn that cool thing into the base of a lamp. And that? I've had it since I was nine years old. I can't get rid of it now.*

As I said, their simple advice made no sense for the way my brain worked. I knew my way of thinking was probably silly, wasteful, and irrational, but could I help it if I was creative and thought outside the box and saw possibilities where others saw junk? Sorry, but their "if this, then that" way of thinking simply didn't cut it as far as I was concerned.

Realization 2—Housekeeping Is a Talent

On the heels of that realization came an even more shocking thought: *Is it possible that housekeeping is a talent, something people are born with—or not?*

Certainly, all the authors of those books seemed to have some sort of natural instinct for the topic. And I knew plenty of people who seemed gifted at this stuff, who seemed to keep their homes clean almost effortlessly, who couldn't understand why I always struggled.

Yes! That had to be it. Housekeeping was a talent. That had to be what was different here between the authors of all of those books and me. Housekeeping talent was what they all had in droves—and what I had not one speck of at all. Not even a smidge. In fact, if those people could be called housekeeping gifted, I was the very opposite of that. I was housekeeping *impaired*.

Nothing about maintaining order in my home came naturally to me. Nothing was done by instinct. Like an aspiring artist who can't draw a decent picture or a basketball wannabe who can't even dribble a ball without tripping, I was incapable of doing what needed to be done because I simply didn't have the talent required.

Realization 3—It's Not My Fault

This was quickly followed by another startling thought. *If housekeeping is a talent, and I just happened to be born without any, then the fact that I struggled in this area was not my fault.* I had to say that one several times out loud, just to hear it and believe it.

Not my fault. My disaster of a home was not my fault. My years of failure were not my fault.

Yet if that was the case, then why did I feel so bad about myself? If I were tone deaf and sang off-key, no one would blame me for that. No one would click their tongue in disgust or make me feel ashamed or think me less of a woman, wife, or mother. They would just know that singing was a talent I didn't possess. So why should cleaning be any different? If it, too, was a talent I didn't possess, where was the shame in that?

With a gasp, I finally understood: There *was* no shame in that! It really wasn't my fault.

It's almost impossible to describe the relief that came flooding into my heart at that moment. After years of self-recrimination and abject humiliation, the understanding that my inadequacies as a housekeeper had nothing to do with any personal character flaws washed over my wounded soul like a balm. In an instant all the lies people like me live with every day—that we just don't care enough or try hard enough or want it bad enough—washed away, leaving peace and self-acceptance in their wake.

Not to confuse things by jumping too far ahead in my tale, but nowadays, when I speak to groups about this book, I see this same reaction all over the room when I get to this point. I see tears, lots of tears. I see nodding heads. I see the same emotions I was feeling when I came to this realization. Trust me, my friend. It's not my fault; it's not your fault. Housekeeping is a talent, and unfortunately for us, it's a talent we just don't happen to have. Let that truth heal your pain as it did mine.

Realization 4—I Can Deal with This Rationally

Once I understood that, my next epiphany was not far behind: *Because my failures in this area are not my fault, then that means I can take the emotion out of the issue and deal with it rationally.*

This particular realization ended up being a much more important one than I recognized at the time, because oh, what progress can be made when bad emotions are stripped away and an issue can be faced with logic and a cool head instead. Suddenly, despair evaporates. Optimism takes hold. Ideas emerge. The moment you take out the guilt and shame, it's as if a big cloud dissipates, revealing more clarity and hope and potential solutions than you ever knew possible. Before you can blink, all sorts of problem-solving strengths begin bubbling to the surface.

Realization 5—I Have Other Talents

Which brings me to realization 5: *Even if I lack a talent for housekeeping, I do have plenty of other talents, some of which I can use for conquering the mess.*

Huh?

I'll say it again.

Even if you are housekeeping impaired, all is not lost. You possess numerous *other* skills that will allow you to circumvent your lack of natural housekeeping abilities and achieve victory over chaos anyway.

Are you imaginative? Energetic? Resourceful? Whatever unique traits you possess, you might be surprised to learn how they can be used to help you achieve a House That Cleans Itself—whether those skills seem to have anything to do with cleaning or not. It has been my observation that the kind of people who tend to be messy are also often clever, creative, and flexible—all qualities that can be used in very unique ways to create cleanliness in a home.

As it turns out, my ability to think outside of the box has been my best ally in fighting mess. Do you see the irony here? For years I assumed this tendency of mine was one of the biggest contributors to my problem. (To wit, my clinging to clutter for the sake of a potential turtle costume.) Yet this tendency has also turned out to be my saving grace.

You also have plenty of qualities that are going to help you in this fight. The key is in finding ways to use these various skills to your advantage as you create a House That Cleans Itself.

And that's good news, especially in light of the next realization.

Realization 6—Everyone Needs a System

See, here's the thing. A baseball player who repeatedly strikes out can always quit the team. A bad singer can always resign from the choir. But a person who is housekeeping impaired still has to manage their stuff as they go through life. With few exceptions, no one can avoid the basics of cleaning. Thus comes realization 6: *Everyone has to find a way to keep their world clean and in order, even those who are housekeeping impaired.*

And therein lies the conundrum.

Because I've always known this, I've spent a lifetime thinking my only option was to change myself. To try harder. To do better. To learn new behaviors.

But once I realized that my problem wasn't a matter of laziness or lack of discipline or some other personal shortcoming that could be repaired but instead was simply a lack of talent, I finally understood that no matter how badly I might want to, I was never going to change, at least not by much. I have always been this way. I am always going to be this way.

Bummer, right? No! Because that's when the biggest puzzle piece of all finally clicked into place.

Realization 7— The Cornerstone of the HTCI System

Here's how my thinking went in that life-changing moment: *I can't change myself. But I do want a clean home, so obviously something has to change. And if I can't change myself, but something has to change, then what else is there? What can I change that will fix this problem?*

As I studied my surroundings—at the piles, the mess, the overwhelming loads of stuff—the strangest thought popped into my mind: *Change the house.*

Immediately, the hairs on the back of my neck began to stand on end. The house? What difference would that make?

Change the house, I told myself again. *Instead of trying to change myself, which I already know doesn't work, change the surroundings. Change this home.*

I can't explain it, but as I looked around, I knew immediately that I was onto something. I was already well aware that our closets were illogically organized, that many of our drawers were too full to be useful. That we had countertops cluttered with things we rarely had need for.

With great clarity, I suddenly realized that such issues made it very difficult for us to do the "clean thing." All over our house, in fact, it was really easy for us to be messy and really hard to be neat. I began to see that because of my housekeeping impairment I had set up my entire home in a way that *discouraged* cleanliness and *encouraged* disaster and chaos.

I began to move through each room, gazing at everything with new eyes. I saw...

...stacks of papers that were never put away *because my filing systems were too complicated.*

...stuff that was never thrown out *because there weren't enough trash cans—and the few cans we did have were too small and inconveniently placed.*

...clothes that lay in heaps all over the bedroom *because the only other option I'd given myself was to put them on hangers and squeeze them into an already overfull closet.*

...toys that littered the floor of rooms where they were played with *because the toy boxes they belonged in were in other rooms too far away.*

...bags of documents in the home office that never seemed to get shredded *because the shredder was in the garage and too hard to get to.*

...bedrooms that were rarely vacuumed *because the vacuum cleaner was heavy and hard to get up the stairs.*

...and on and on.

My house was a constant mess because in my impairment I had made it too hard to keep it clean. It was that simple. I had engineered disaster from the get-go.

Turning that realization on its ear, I asked myself the obvious question: *If a person could engineer disaster, could they not also engineer cleanliness?*

Of course they could! Naturally neat people did it every day without even realizing it. It's just that for someone like me, it would have to be a more conscious process. It would have to be done with thought, planning, and intention.

And this was realization 7, the most important revelation of all: *Instead of trying to change myself, which has never worked anyway, I need to change my house. I need to turn it into a home that lends itself to cleanliness instead of messiness.*

With that thought in mind, I moved back through each room, this time with an eye toward problem solving.

Change the house. Change the house.

Okay. So, what if I...

...got a second vacuum cleaner, one that stayed upstairs all the time? *Then I wouldn't have to lug the heavy one up and down, and I'd be more likely to vacuum the bedrooms more often.*

...moved the shredder out of the garage and into the home office? *Then the shredding would actually get done whenever it needed to rather than building up into big bags of mess.*

...relocated those toy boxes to more convenient areas, so the toys would be easier to put away? *Then the kids might be more likely to do so without being asked—or at least without being nagged a dozen times.*

...got rid of some of the clothes in my closet, put up some pegs and hooks, and got a big basket or two to hold any overflow? *Then my room wouldn't constantly look like the donation area for a secondhand clothing store.*

...put a trash can in every single room of our home? *Then all over the house, those little scraps of paper and broken toys and torn off labels and more would be thrown away immediately rather than piled up on tables and shelves until cleaning day, as they had always been before.*

...came up with a much easier, more logical filing system? *Then I'd be far more likely to actually file away my papers rather than just leave them in massive piles.*

And so on.

What a moment. What a day. What a beginning of our new life of clean.

Truly, I had seen the light.

Of course, the changes I thought of that first day were not humongous ones. For the most part, they didn't require a ton of money. They didn't take a brain surgeon to implement. They were, in fact, the kinds of commonsense steps a person who is housekeeping gifted would have done in the first place without even thinking about it.

But not me. No, not me, not the housekeeping-impaired woman who had struggled valiantly for years with the best of intentions but the worst of instincts.

Oh, how I had sabotaged myself! How I had made our lives so much more difficult than they needed to be. If only I had known there really *was* a way to have a clean house that had nothing to do with self discipline or trying harder or wanting it more or any of those other lies that I'd bought into for so many years.

A part of me wanted to weep, but a bigger part of me rejoiced.

I was ready to put the past behind me, move forward, and fix this problem in a whole new and unconventional way. It was time to go from realizations to reality.

My Most Embarrassing Messy House Story
—To Tell the Truth—
BY JASON L.

During the Children's Chat at our church, the pastor asked the kids what they usually did to help out around the house when it was time to clean. One bright youngster raised his hand and announced, "I pick up all the empties."

Needless to say the parents were mortified, but the rest of the congregation had a good laugh!

3

From Realization to Reality

Forget the former things; do not dwell on the past.
See, I am doing a new thing!

Isaiah 43:18-19

Once I had my life-changing series of epiphanies, I set about turning those thoughts into actions. Like the heroines in my books, I decided to become a detective of sorts as I studied and dissected our messes and diagnosed the issues that were creating clutter and chaos throughout our home. After I identified the causes, I tried to come up with solutions and alternatives, using logic, common sense, and lots of creative problem solving.

At first I didn't tell a soul what I was doing. I didn't know if my plan would work or not, but I wanted to give it a shot without input or skepticism or nay-saying. I didn't even tell my husband—not because I feared he'd squash my hopes (he's not that kind of guy), but because I didn't want to get *his* hopes up only to see my grand plan fail in the end.

Thus I worked alone, starting at one end of my house and slowly moving toward the other, experimenting and implementing, weeding out and rearranging, thinking and trying, and slowly fixing what was wrong. My goal throughout was to make it as easy to do the neat thing as it was to do the messy thing, all over the house. I also gave a lot of thought to various tricks and techniques that would lend an overall feeling of clean, from analyzing each room's first impression to focusing on

camouflage and more. Room by room, I converted my illogically organized, prone-to-fall-apart home into one that would stay clean in a way
that made sense for our lifestyle, our behaviors, our habits.

Of course, my family noticed certain changes, but they just thought
it was Mom doing her thing, a little mindless rearranging like always.
They didn't recognize that my efforts were very intentional this time,
each change one part of a much bigger picture.

By the time I was finished, the house looked great. But it wasn't
just clean. This time, it *stayed* clean. Day after day after day. The longer
that clean lasted, the more I allowed myself to hope. That hope grew
every time I walked from room to room without having to flinch or veer
around piles or feel that familiar flush of shame as I surveyed what lay in
front of me. Our home wasn't magazine photo ready, perhaps, but it was
people ready. It was clean enough that we no longer tripped over our
stuff, lost things on a regular basis, or felt ourselves smothered in mess
and overwhelmed. Best of all, with very little effort, once the house got
that way, it stayed that way. And stayed that way. And stayed that way.

Then came the moment my husband finally put it into words.

I was telling him about a conversation with a friend who had com-
mented on how consistently clean our home had been lately.

He nodded. "She's right. This place has been staying so neat, it's
almost like the house is cleaning itself."

I grinned, thrilled that my amazing new housekeeping system
finally had a name. The House That Cleans Itself? Precisely.

The House That Cleans Itself, Version 2.0

As I said in chapter 1, once I'd spread the word a bit and tested out
my plan on others, I decided to put my system into a book. The original release of *The House That Cleans Itself* centered around what I call
the CONVERT system, a specific-but-time-consuming step-by-step
approach for turning your messy home into a House That Cleans Itself.

Since that book came out a few years ago, I have continued to hone
and polish the system in my own house through ongoing trial and error.

I have also received feedback from countless others across the country and around the world, learning what works and what doesn't for them. Through all of this I've come to realize that having a House That Cleans Itself is not so much about following a step-by-step conversion to the letter as it is about embracing a completely new way of thinking and acting when it comes to one's home and possessions.

Put simply, the plan is far more flexible than I originally thought. It can be implemented on the grand scale presented in the original book, yes, but also in smaller, less drastic ways. Either method, large or small, still adds up to huge differences in the long run, contributing greatly to the overall cleanliness of a home.

I've also come to realize that this plan isn't just for disastrous homes, like mine used to be, but for homes all across the spectrum of cleanliness. Some of my most enthusiastic reader mail, in fact, has been from those who used the system to solve one or two problem areas in an otherwise tidy home.

Certainly, my original approach worked, but what I've learned is that I could make this plan even easier to implement. And if there's one thing the housekeeping impaired need, it's an easier way to do anything household related.

Because of that, when I learned this book would be rereleased, I knew I wanted to do some restructuring first. Though I would retain much of the same helpful information, I was eager to present that information in a way that was easier to follow, faster to implement, and much more accessible to all. To my great joy, the publisher agreed. Thus, the book you're now holding in your hand really is a new and improved version of the original—better, easier, and more complete than ever before. Think of it as *The House That Cleans Itself*, version 2.0.

This time, instead of shaping the book around the CONVERT system, I have taken the simpler approach of focusing on the eight fundamental steps to a House That Cleans Itself.

As you put these eight steps into practice in your home, you'll see it begin to grow cleaner—and then *stay* cleaner—than ever before.

The Eight Steps of the HTCI System

The eight steps will each have their own chapter, but for summary purposes, these steps are:

1. *Become a detective.* By gathering evidence throughout your home and then analyzing that evidence, you'll learn what your various problem areas and messes consist of and exactly what's causing them to happen.

2. *Change the house to fit the behavior.* Once you've tracked down the root causes of mess, you'll learn how to use creative problem solving to make changes—not to yourself, but to your *house*. These changes, if done correctly, will keep your home neater and cleaner than ever before.

3. *Create a first impression of clean.* By employing several clever techniques, you can enhance the immediate "cleanliness factor" of every room in your home, which in turn boosts morale, leads to neater behaviors, and reinforces the main principles of the House That Cleans Itself System.

4. *Think like a hotel.* Take a cue from the hotel industry and learn numerous ways to streamline the cleaning process. For example, make changes to your home so that it will end up doing some of the cleaning work *for* you.

5. *Aim for simplicity.* From furniture choices to quantity of possessions, simplicity rules in a House That Cleans Itself. The cold, hard truth is that no home can be consistently clean if it contains too much stuff. This chapter helps you deal with releasing your clutter—not by offering up the same old rules of thumb about how to ditch your stuff, but by providing a new and unconventional method for facing this issue in a way that should finally make sense for you and how your mind works.

6. *Explore the "why."* There are reasons you may have trouble keeping your house clean—such as an "all or nothing" tendency toward cleaning or an "out of sight, out of mind" issue—and often simply by understanding these reasons, you can find clever ways to work around them and keep your home clean regardless.

7. *Make it a team effort.* Unless you live alone, it's important to learn

how to involve the whole family in implementing and maintaining the HTCI System in your home. Even if you face family-related cleaning issues, such as a reluctant spouse or less-than-enthusiastic children, this step will show you how to get everyone on board for your own House That Cleans Itself.

8. *Put God at the center.* This important step helps you to put your home in God's hands and make Him the center of your housecleaning efforts. He has much better uses for your time and resources than shuffling around a bunch of possessions, dust, and junk. Once you've achieved your House That Cleans Itself, you'll have new freedom to focus on His blessings and explore the life He intends for you to live.

A Dose of Reality

Before moving on to the first step, I'd like to share a brief but true tale that should serve as an encouragement as you embark on this exciting new adventure of clean.

In the spring of 2000, I had a part-time temporary job that involved going door to door throughout numerous Pennsylvania neighborhoods. Over the course of that job, I visited about 300 houses located in five different middle- to upper-middle-class towns in two different counties. And though my work had nothing whatsoever to do with housekeeping, I couldn't help but take note of some amazing statistics.

Of those 300 or so homes where I arrived unannounced and unexpected and went inside, exactly three—yes, *three*—were perfectly, spotlessly clean.

Out of the rest:

+ about 10 percent were somewhat messy but livable (the main living areas could have been cleaned up in about 10 to 15 minutes)

+ about 40 percent were very messy (the main living areas could have been cleaned up in about 1 to 3 hours)

+ about 50 percent were so messy there wasn't anywhere to sit down

I kid you not. *Half* of those homes were such a disaster we had to stand the entire time we filled out the forms.

As you can imagine, that experience was a real eye-opener for me. For some reason, I thought every other house was spotless and ours was the only messy one. I'm not sure where I got that notion, but I have to guess it came from a combination of TV and magazines, reinforced by visits to friends' and family's homes, which always seemed far, far neater than mine. But showing up unannounced and catching home-owners by surprise provided a far more realistic picture of what's really going on behind closed doors. People are messy. Life is messy.

I wasn't nearly as alone as I thought—and neither are you.

For some reason, whenever I share this story at a House That Cleans Itself event, the crowd goes a little bit crazy, every bit as shocked and excited by these findings as I was. I'm not sure why, but they, too, seem encouraged by this news.

My friend, no matter where your home falls on the clean spectrum, rest assured that you are not alone, not by a long shot. We've all struggled with mess to some extent or another. But now that you hold this book in your hands, you hold the information you need to put that struggle to an end for good. Are you ready to turn your home into a House That Cleans Itself? Then let's get started.

As the saying goes, every journey begins with the first step.

Part 2

Step into Clean

Wisdom will enter your heart,
and knowledge will be pleasant
to your soul.

Proverbs 2:10

4

Become a Detective

STEP 1

The LORD gives wisdom, and from his mouth come knowledge and understanding.

PROVERBS 2: 6

Like any good detective, your goal for this step is to gather evidence and then use that evidence to figure out the answers to some important questions. Those questions are:

+ What are the problem areas in my home?

+ What items do our recurring messes generally consist of?

+ Why do these particular problems and messes keep happening?

This chapter will describe the best ways to gather that evidence as well as what to look for when you analyze it.

Gather the Evidence

If I were to ask you to name the problem areas in your home, chances are you could easily rattle off a whole laundry list. I'm sure that among the list would be some hints as to the causes as well. For example, "There are always cans and boxes of food on the counter because our pantry's too small," or "We always have junk by the back door because everybody dumps their stuff there when they come in," and so on. We all know the issues in various rooms throughout our homes that bug us. But that's not exactly what we're looking for here.

In the previous chapter I talked about the need to become dispassionate about your mess, to take the emotion out of the equation. I was speaking primarily about ridding yourself of guilt and shame, but now I would add a few more emotions you must rid yourself of as well, including frustration, irritation, anger, and hurt—in short, every other negative feeling that tends to surface whenever you contemplate the messes around your home. Even if you have good cause to feel those ways (an inconsiderate spouse, unreliable children) this isn't the time for playing the blame game. If you want to tackle the mess in a constructive way, right now you need to put aside all negativity and face the situation as devoid of emotion as if this were someone else's home and you were a stranger happening upon it for the very first time.

You'll need to gather a few tools, including:

+ a stepladder or low stool you can easily carry from room to room

+ a camera, preferably digital so you can see your photos right away

+ a pen or pencil

+ blank paper or photocopies of the Evidence Record form found in the back of this book. (You can also download and print a PDF version of this form from the House That Cleans Itself page on my website at www.mindy starnsclark.com.)

Once you have the correct tools, it's Nancy Drew time. What you're going to do is choose a room or area of your home, go there, and evaluate it for cleanliness. Try to work from pure observation rather than memory, as if you are a stranger here. As you look around, what do you see? Where are the biggest messes? In general, what items do those messes consist of?

As if you're making notes at a crime scene, take stock of all you see and record those findings in a list, either on a blank page or on a copy of the Evidence Record form. Be specific.

Let's say you're analyzing the great room in your home, which consists of the kitchen, the family room, and the main entryway. You may start by writing, *Pile of clutter to left of door.* But then under that, specify what the clutter consists of. For example:

+ counter beside door covered with papers for school, keys, library books and DVDs, gloves and scarves, coins, map, political flyer that had been left on doorknob

+ floor beside door littered with shoes, backpacks, gym bag, baseball mitt

Continuing on through the great room area by area, write down any other messes you see, breaking them down into detail as well. This evidence-gathering mission may uncover such issues as:

+ coats and jackets left on the coatrack after the season is over

+ magnets and papers cluttering up the front of fridge

+ stuff from interrupted projects left on the table and mixing in with other stuff

+ groceries, especially bulk items, left on the kitchen counter

+ containers holding items that ought to go in cabinets or drawers or on shelves but instead have been left out

+ cleaning products sitting out where they were used

+ stuff piled on the floor because it has nowhere else to go

+ stuff piled at bottom of stairs waiting to go up

+ "extras" of items currently in use: extra purses, jackets, sports equipment, and more

- ✦ trash that didn't make it to the trash can
- ✦ items that need to be thrown away: empty pill bottles, boxes from mail, packaging from items purchased
- ✦ exercise equipment, such as balls, rackets, and pads
- ✦ jumbles of wires near computer, appliances, and other electronics
- ✦ DVDs, videos, and games on the floor near the television
- ✦ books and magazines already read or looked through
- ✦ stuff waiting to be given away or donated
- ✦ holiday decorations missed when packed up from the last holiday (or the one before that)

Even if your home is relatively clean, you may spot at least some of the above problems, any one of which can contribute to an overall feeling of mess—but that can easily be prevented in a House That Cleans Itself.

Now it's time to take one more look at the same space from a new perspective, which is what the stepladder is for. It's human nature to stop seeing what's in front of us all the time, so the point here is to jolt your usual perspective and allow yourself to see with fresh eyes. Place the stepladder or stool in the center of the room, climb up on it, and then look down from a bird's-eye view to see if you notice anything else contributing to the mess you haven't already recorded on your list. Be sure to keep an eye open for anything less obvious that might also be contributing to an overall feeling of disorder or disrepair, such as stains, tears, rust, frayed edges, and dirty fingerprints.

Write down any additional findings this new perspective reveals, for example:

- ✦ dirty footprints by door
- ✦ doormat askew and looks messy
- ✦ fingerprints all over mirror beside door
- ✦ plant in corner wilting and ugly

When you feel your list is complete, there's one more evidence-gathering task to do: Take out the camera and snap some photos of the room. Don't be embarrassed even if what you're capturing through that lens is disastrous. You'll need these photos to help with the process, but there are two other reasons that make them worth doing as well. We'll get to those in chapter 18, "Mind over Matter," but for now let's just focus on biting the bullet and snapping away.

When you're finished, upload your photos to your computer or have them developed and then study each picture with your list in hand. More than likely you'll notice one or two more things contributing to the mess you didn't spot with your naked eye. (Again, it's all about seeing the familiar from a new perspective.) Add these observations to the list. Now it's time to analyze what you've found.

Analyze the Evidence

I always thought of the messes in my home as unpredictable, as if their appearance and content were random and ever changing. But once I embarked on this new approach to housekeeping and began to study the contents and causes of the various piles and collections throughout my house, I was surprised to realize that most messes weren't random at all. They were, in fact, usually quite predictable and consistent.

Right now, as you read through the list you just made, you're probably drawing the same conclusion. The individual elements of those messes may vary from week to week, but chances are the *nature* of the items contributing to that mess are essentially the same. And that's good news for anyone who wants a cleaner home, because every mess that has a definable cause will also have a logical solution. The first step as you analyze the evidence, then, is to try to define the nature of the items cropping up in any given area, because what we're trying to get to here is the *root cause* behind the mess.

Consider that pile of clutter by the front door, described above. Almost every item in that pile is something that was either on its way in or on its way out—*papers for school, keys, library books and DVDs, gloves and scarves, coins, map, political flyer, shoes, backpacks, gym bag,* and *catcher's mitt.* These things ended up beside the door either because someone put them there as they came in or because someone put them there to take with them for when they go back out. Clearly, there's nothing random about this mess at all, even if the individual items differ somewhat from week to week. The root cause is easy to discern: This family doesn't have a good system for dealing with the items related to the ins and outs of daily life.

Thus, if you broke it down into columns, your list might end up looking like this:

Evidence	Reason	Root cause
Pile of clutter to left of front door: papers for school, keys, library books and DVDs, gloves and scarves, coins, map, political flyer left on doorknob, shoes, backpacks, gym bags, and *sports equipment*	Because someone either put these things there as they came in or put them there to take with them when they go back out.	Because we don't have a good system for dealing with the items related to the ins and outs of daily life.

For the other issues in that area, you might write:

Evidence	Reason	Root cause
Dirty footprints by door	Somebody tracked in mud.	Our doormat situation is not sufficient for our needs.

Doormat askew and looks messy	People accidentally kick it as they pass through.	The doormat is old and has lost the rubbery backing that keeps it in place.
Fingerprints all over mirror beside door	When people come inside, their hands hit the mirror and leave prints as they're fumbling for the light switch.	The mirror is hanging too close to the light switch.
Plant in corner wilting and ugly	We keep forgetting to water it.	We need a better system for plant care.

In the examples of messes in other parts of the house, a breakdown of some of the evidence might look like this:

Evidence	Reason	Root cause
Stuff from interrupted project left on table and got mixed in with other stuff	Thought for sure I'd get back to that soon but then I didn't, and other things we put on the table got all cluttered together.	I don't have a "temporary storage place" for putting projects that get interrupted.
Magnets and papers cluttering up front of fridge	Those papers are important reminders and have to go somewhere so we can see them on a regular basis.	We need a better place to put important papers where we'll notice them but they won't look so messy.

Groceries, especially bulk items, left on the kitchen counter	No time to do it when I first got home from the store, and then I never got around to it later.	I don't have anywhere else less noticeable to stash nonperishable groceries temporarily till I can put them away where they belong.
Coats and jackets left on the coatrack after the season is over	Time got away from me, and I didn't notice they were still there.	We don't have a reminder system in place for seasonal clothing maintenance.
Jumbles of wires near computer and appliances	I never noticed before so never did anything about it.	I don't have a good way to handle cord clutter.

You get the idea. For every single messy area in your home, there is usually a simple reason for how it got that way and an easily discernible root cause for what's creating that problem in the first place. As you go through your list, write down the reason and root cause for every single item on it.

You may already have a good feel for how the next step will play out. Now that you have an issue, a reason, and a root cause, it's time to come up with some solutions and implement them, which is where the fun really begins.

My Most Embarrassing Messy House Story
—A Hidden Unmentionable—
BY BETH

Several weeks after my teenage daughter had a sleepover, we found her friend's bra under the sofa. I don't know who was more embarrassed, the girl for losing it or me for not vacuuming under the sofa for so long.

5

Change the House to Fit the Behavior

STEP 2

There is a time for everything,
and a season for every activity under the heavens...
a time to search and a time to give up,
a time to keep and a time to throw away.

ECCLESIASTES 3:1,6

Now that you've tracked down the root causes of your messes, it's time to take things to the next logical conclusion and use creative problem solving to make changes—not to yourself, but to your home. The right kinds of changes made throughout each room will eventually lead to an entire House That Cleans Itself.

When faced with a mess, most ordinary cleaning books may simply tell you to do a better job of putting those items away where they belong—"a place for everything and everything in its place"—perhaps by providing handy tips for an efficient cleaning schedule or nifty tricks that will get your kids up and cleaning alongside you. But that kind of advice only works for those who are naturally gifted at this stuff. For the housekeeping impaired, it's just not that simple. Some items have never been given a place at all, and even for the items that do have a place, chances are those places are so illogical and poorly chosen that using them on a regular basis has simply become more trouble than it's worth.

In other words, even if you do get the stuff put away today, the same mess is only going to accumulate again later because you haven't done anything to fix the root problem. Like slapping a bandage on an infected wound, you've solved nothing beyond the immediate situation.

In a House That Cleans Itself, however, the goal is to find solutions for the root causes of recurring messes so that they'll stop happening once and for all. The reason this approach is so effective is because by relocating where things belong to more logical and convenient locations, you'll find that you're making it just as easy to do the neat thing as it is to do the messy one. You've engineered cleaning convenience, which is one of the primary goals of every House That Cleans Itself.

Consider the very first real HTCI-type change I made in my own home. I love to tell this story because it's the perfect example of what the House That Cleans Itself System is all about. This was when my daughters were in grade school and one of my biggest sources of daily aggravation was their backpacks. Every day after getting off the bus, they would come in the front door and dump their backpacks the moment they stepped inside. The sight of those grungy, messy backpacks plopped there in our front hallway for all to see simply drove me crazy. It didn't matter that the backpacks belonged around the corner, in the dining room, where they were less visible. It didn't matter that I had nagged, cajoled, punished, pleaded, and fussed for years, insisting that they not drop those packs until they had walked around to where they belonged. Almost every day my kids continued to step inside, dump their stuff at the door, and head on into the house.

Let me just say that these were not bad children. They were for the most part very well behaved, very considerate. But there was something about the whole backpack deal that eluded every behavioral modification trick I could come up with. Had they been spoiled or lazy or disobedient in other ways, then that would have been a different matter. But in the case of the messy backpacks, their bad behavior was neither willful nor malicious. The best I could figure, it was born of distraction and exhaustion. By the time they had made it through an entire day of school and a long bus ride home, the only thoughts on their mind were *snack* and *flop*. I honestly believe that as they stepped through that door, they were just so glad to be home—and so tired of lugging around 20 to 30 pounds of canvas-enclosed books and notebooks, that it was all they could do not to collapse there on the floor alongside their packs.

That's why, after years of trying to get them to "do better," I decided it was time to come up with a radical new solution that would work for all of us, one that wouldn't require them to change their behavior—which we'd already seen was a losing battle. I was going to tackle this issue the House That Cleans Itself way.

The evidence, of course, was *backpacks cluttering floor beside front door,* and the reason was *kids won't put them away where they belong.* At first, I listed the root cause as *they are too distracted and exhausted to do it when they first get home,* but the more I thought about it, the more I could see the fallacy in that thinking. If I was going to change the house to fit the behavior, then we needed to change the place where the backpacks belonged. Even though it shouldn't have been that big of a deal—around the corner and into the dining room was only about fifteen feet away—the real reason the backpacks weren't getting put away was because *the place they're supposed to go is too far away from where they keep trying to put them.*

The problem was that no storage opportunities existed closer to the door, no closets or cabinets in which to stash the packs. There was, however, a little bit of extra space—perhaps a foot wide by three feet long—where I might be able to squeeze something in. After much thought and shopping around, I finally came home with a wooden bench that also served as a trunk.

I put it in place while the kids were still at school one day, thrilled to see that it fit and looked okay. Not great, but certainly better than a pile of dirty backpacks. Besides, I decided, not only would my new bench hide those packs, it would do double duty as a place to sit and put on shoes before heading out the door.

That afternoon, I couldn't wait for them to get home from school.

Shortly before the bus was to arrive, I propped open the trunk. When they came inside, they started to drop their packs but then froze with them in midair. I met their startled expressions with a grin.

"Go ahead," I said, "drop your backpacks as usual. Drop 'em right there inside that trunk."

Barely having to move a single step, my two children did as I said, placing their packs exactly where they always had. But this time, once those packs were down, all we had to do was close the lid of that trunk, and suddenly the mess was out of sight.

Voilà. With very little effort on their part or mine, my entryway looked perfectly neat—even though almost nothing had changed about my children's behavior. They still walked in the door and dumped their packs right there where they stood. Yet because I had made a change to the house, that behavior no longer created a mess.

If you're naturally gifted at housekeeping, right now you are probably rolling your eyes or scratching your head and going, "Uh, yeah!" But if you're housekeeping impaired, you're more than likely nodding and smiling and saying, "Of course. This makes such sense. Eureka!"

My fellow impaired ones, this is exactly what I'm talking about when I say *change the house to fit the behavior.* It may sound ridiculously simple, but if you can tackle the messes throughout your home in a similar way—figuring out what the problems are and then coming up with solutions to fix those problems once and for all, as we'll explore in this chapter—eventually your house will be transformed into one that stays neater and cleaner than ever before.

Remember: Changes made to a behavior are almost never permanent, but changes made to a house will last forever—or at least for as long as you want them to.

Finding Solutions

Creative problem solving requires you to look at things in a whole new way. It involves thinking outside of the box, allowing yourself to be unconventional, opening your mind to brainstorming, and idea sharing. The goal is to find good, logical, working solutions for the root causes of your household messes, even if some of those solutions sound a little bit wacky. It's best to come up with a range of ideas and then narrow them down from there. It can take a bit of experimenting and tweaking to figure out which solution will be the best choice, but it's worth the trouble because if you do, then eventually most of the biggest messes in your home can be eliminated—permanently.

Consider one of the issues described in the previous chapter:

> *Stuff from interrupted project left on table and got mixed in with other stuff.*

We already determined the reason:

> *Thought for sure I'd get back to that pretty soon but then I didn't, and other things we put on the table got all cluttered together.*

We also identified the root cause:

> *I don't have a "temporary storage place" for projects that get interrupted.*

Now it's time to brainstorm some solutions, for example:

> *Keep a big, empty bin handy whenever I do a project, and if I have to move on to something else before I'm done, take a minute to remove everything from the table and stick it in the bin, where it can safely stay till you're I'm to work on it again.*

This solution is a start but it isn't perfect because it requires the extra steps of keeping a big, empty bin handy and removing everything from the table into the bin if necessary. It also might prove frustrating for projects that don't "dismantle" easily. Another solution might be:

> *Get a big tray, and every time I do a project put that tray down first and do everything on the tray. Then, if I don't finish, all I have to do to clear the table is pick up the tray and carry it some-where else out of the way.*

Certainly, this approach would prevent the need for dismantling. On the other hand, it would only work in a home where there's room enough "somewhere else out of the way" to store the project tray when not in use. For a truly radical solution along these same lines, you might even consider the following solution, which I developed for this problem in my home office:

I got the idea one time while standing in a Krispy Kreme shop, watching the donut-making process through the window. As donuts came off the conveyor belt, they were placed on a large plastic tray. Each time a tray was full, the attendant would carry it to a nearby rack, slide it into place, and take out the next tray. Seeing this, it struck me that

I could handle the projects in my office somewhat the same way with a sturdy baker's rack (also called a "jelly rack" or "donut rack") from a local restaurant supply store. Rather than using file folders (which don't work for me) or project lists (which I know I'll lose), I put each ongoing project onto a separate tray of that rack. Now if I want to create a newsletter or do research for a book or write an article or press release, I simply pull the corresponding tray from the rack and carry it to my desk.

Of course, if space isn't an issue in your home, then the ultimate solution would be:

> Create a project area in a different room where anything left unfinished after one sitting will be left alone until I can get back to it.

Still not a viable solution for you? Then keep brainstorming, and I'm sure you'll come up with even more ideas about how to handle this issue. The solution you'll want to end up choosing depends on the space in your home, the frequency with which you do projects, and the types of projects you do. As you weigh your options, there are two rules to keep in mind. These are:

1. The solution has to work for *you* and the way you think and behave.

2. The problem *must* be dealt with and not ignored. Don't brush it aside with a quick, "I just won't let that happen again." Of *course* you will! You're *you*. You need to be realistic, face facts, and then come up with a way to preempt this sort of mess in the future so that it won't ever happen again.

More Creative Problem Solving

To reinforce this principle of changing the house to fit the behavior, let's consider another example. One of the issues listed the previous chapter was:

Groceries, especially bulk items, left on the kitchen counter.

We already determined the reason:

No time to do it when I first got home from the store, and then I never got around to it later.

And we identified the root cause:

Don't have anywhere else less noticeable to stash nonperishable groceries temporarily till I can put them away where they belong.

A cleaning expert would probably have a fit with this one. "You want a place to temporarily stash your groceries? Are you kidding me? Just suck it up and put them away as soon as you get home."

That may work for them, but it's not the reality in my house, and it may not be in yours either. The fact is, I frequently used to end up with groceries sitting on the counter after my shopping trips—and they would often stay there for several days before finally migrating to their proper place. Sometimes it was more a matter of exhaustion than time constraints. After a big shopping trip, I was just too tired to put everything away right then. I would get the stuff in the fridge and freezer, of course, but beyond that, the rest could wait.

Still, no one wants boxes and cans cluttering their counters, so what's a body to do? One possible solution might be to *delegate*. Perhaps the one who does the shopping and the one who puts the food away should be two different people. The chore of "putting away the groceries" could go on the list of any child who is big enough to reach the cabinets. This was the final solution in our house.

If you have no one to delegate to, or if you prefer to put the groceries away yourself, then another option might be to *establish a "temp zone,"* such as a big basket or an area of cabinet or pantry space, for just this purpose. Don't forget to put away perishables first, but then shove everything else into that designated temp zone before you leave the kitchen. Just be sure to set a limit on how long items can remain there until you come back and put them where they really belong, or you're going to end up wasting a lot of effort trying to find what you need every time you cook.

You might even consider installing a pull-down door or shade underneath the kitchen cabinets mounted above your countertops, and use it to create an instant hiding space, behind which you tuck the groceries out of sight. The good thing about this solution is that it lends itself to a natural time limit. The resulting loss of counter space is just frustrating enough that you'll get around to putting away those hidden groceries sooner rather than later.

If neither of these suggestions work for you or your home, you might consider taking a second look at the reason and root cause you came up with in the first step. Though this may not have registered consciously, perhaps the real reason you've had trouble getting your groceries fully put away is because:

Your pantry is already full. Sometimes we avoid putting away the groceries because we know the stuff won't all fit. If that's the problem in your home, you have two choices: Get more food storage space or store less food. Only you know which is your particular problem. Is your pantry big enough yet always full? Then it's time to do an inventory, toss the items that have expired, give away the ones you're never going to cook with, and start creating the next month's menus around the food that is left. Work down that surplus until a too-stuffed pantry is no longer an issue.

Is your pantry too small for the number of people you have to feed? Then take a look around and see if you can come up with more food storage space. Make sure it's convenient and logical, and then do what you need to do to expand into that space as well.

Your pantry is a big mess. Sometimes we avoid putting away the groceries because we fear that the new stuff is only going to get lost in there. If this is your situation, clear out that pantry, decide on categories, label the shelves, and get organized. It's not fun, but once in a while it's necessary. And because you'll be living in a House That Cleans Itself, what you'll find is that once you change the house (organize the pantry) then your mess-inducing behavior (leaving the groceries out on the counter instead of putting them away) is likely to disappear without your even realizing it.

Your pantry is too organized. Sometimes we avoid putting away the groceries because we let our tendency to over-categorize get away with us. If this is something you've done in your pantry, then putting food away can be such a mental challenge that you avoid it entirely. If this is your situation, remove those labels and try again with more general categories. For example, rather than dividing your cans out into twelve different categories (cream-based soups, broth-based soups, green vegetables, beans), allow yourself only three categories (soups, fruits and vegetables, and other). Once putting away your food no longer requires mental gymnastics, you'll be far more likely to do it in a timely manner.

Sometimes doing this step is simply a matter of finding the right solution, and sometimes it's a matter of reevaluating the reasons and root cause behind the problem. Either way, the more you can *remove* emotion from the equation, *think* outside the box, *persist* until you come up with solutions that will work for you and the way you think, and *force* yourself to deal with each mess-inducing problem as a house issue rather than a behavior issue, the sooner you'll have a House That Cleans Itself.

My Most Embarrassing Messy House Story
—A Telltale Ring—
BY L.W.

Early in my married life I struggled to keep up with three kids and all the housework. Some things had to go. Well, I knew I'd let it go too long when one of my children's friends looked at our bathtub in horror.

"Ewww!" the six-year-old pixie exclaimed as she pointed at the dark ring around the inside of the tub. "My mommy would never let me take a bath in there."

"Oh," my daughter answered, "that's just so we know how far to fill the water."

I slunk away, and from that day on, we never had a ring around our tub again.

6

Create a First Impression of Clean

STEP 3

His eyes are on the ways of mortals;
he sees their every step.

JOB 34:21

This next step involves using several clever techniques to make every room in your home look neater and cleaner at first glance. Though this gives visitors to your home a delightful first impression, the main reason for this step has nothing to do with them and everything to do with you and the others who live there. The instant-cleanliness factor provides a cheery, uplifting sense of order throughout the house, which then leads to naturally neater behaviors and helps reinforces the main principles of the House That Cleans Itself System.

At its core, this step is primarily a mind game. Imagine that you walk into a room where the first thing you see is a table covered with mess. You think, *This room is messy.* Even as you come the rest of the way into the room, take a further look, and see that the only really messy thing is that table, your initial reaction still holds. To your mind, whether consciously or unconsciously, the room is "messy" with "areas of clean." If it's a room you're responsible for, that thought leaves you feeling demoralized, depressed, and defeated.

Imagine, however, walking into a room where the first thing you see is a neat floor and a perfectly made bed. You think, *This room is clean.* Even as you come the rest of the way into the room, take a further look, and see a messy table over in the corner, your initial reaction still holds. To your mind, whether consciously or unconsciously, the room is "clean" with an "area of mess." If it's a room you're responsible for, that thought leaves you feeling pleased, relaxed, and energized. You're also more likely to attack the mess on that table so that the whole room will be as clean as you thought it was when you first looked inside.

I've come up with four tricks for achieving that all-important first impression of clean:

1. Control your sight zones.
2. Corral your necessary messes.
3. Utilize camouflage.
4. Eliminate the inevitable invisibles.

This chapter will take you through each of these four techniques and show you how to put them into practice in your home.

Control Your Sight Zones

A "sight zone" is what I call the area you see when you stand in a doorway and look into a room. For some reason, those of us who are housekeeping impaired rarely give any thought to the cleanliness factor of our sight zones, yet most naturally neat people do so without even realizing it.

Controlling the sight zones throughout your home is one of the best tools in your HTCI toolbox. Engineering your sight zones effectively can make an entire room feel neater and cleaner—whether you actually clean anything in the process or not.

There are three steps to controlling a sight zone:

1. Determine a room's sight zone by standing in the doorway and making note of what part of the room is

most visible to you from that doorway. (A room has as many sight zones as there are doorways.)

2. With regard to the various furnishings and/or areas in the room, make a realistic assessment as to which of these are likely to stay clean more often and which are likely to look messy more often. Be honest about your best and worst cleaning tendencies in that area. Does your dresser top stay messy but you're pretty good about making the bed each day? Do your clothes pile up on the straight-backed chair but the easy chair and the area around it tends to stay relatively empty and uncluttered? The better you can identify these clean and messy areas, the more effectively you can use your sight zones.

3. Wherever possible, rearrange the room so that the areas most likely to stay clean are inside the sight zone and the areas most likely to get messy are outside the sight zone.

Say, for example, that your family tends to be careless when it comes to bookshelves. They grab books and use them, but then they don't put them back as neatly as they should. After a while half of the books are no longer lined up on the shelves but are instead crammed in sideways and stuck in piles. You need to invoke the rule of the sight zone, which states that anything in your home that's likely to get messy over time should be placed outside the sight zone whenever possible. Picture the same room set up two different ways:

When you step into the room on the left, the first thing you see is the bookcase because it is against the wall opposite the door. Thus, if those shelves are messy, your impression of the entire room is that it's messy, even if it's not.

When you step into the room on the right, the bookcase has been placed next to the doorway you're in. To see those messy books, you have to step into the room and turn around. By that time, if the rest of the room is fairly neat, your brain will have already registered "neat." This is how you arrange a room to take advantage of the sight zone principle.

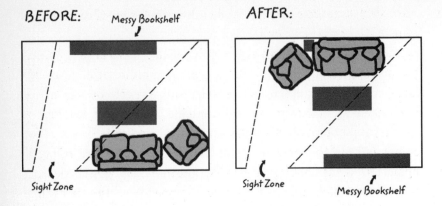

BEFORE: Messy Bookshelf   AFTER:

Sight Zone   Sight Zone   Messy Bookshelf

To maximize this principle throughout your home, think about your family's messiest tendencies and where they most often manifest. Bureau tops, entertainment areas, and open shelving are some of the most likely culprits. Try to locate these out of the main line of sight wherever possible, and you'll lend those rooms a near-instant feeling of clean.

To further draw the eye toward neatness and away from mess, you might also consider adding a focal point of some kind within each sight zone. Just make sure that the focal point you choose is something that will always stay clean and neat, such as a lighted painting that hangs on the wall rather than something that tends to get messy, such as a vividly colored toy shelf. Otherwise it will end up working against you, and you'll be even worse off than when you started.

In many homes, the most difficult view to tackle is the one from the front door. Sometimes a sight zone is too broad, covering so many areas that it's impossible to arrange things so they will look nice all the time. In the suburbs of Philadelphia where I live, the trend with newer homes seems to be toward having front door sight zones that encompass several rooms, including the kitchen and a big family room. If the houses are nicely decorated and perfectly neat, the broad scope of the sight zone is very striking and dramatic. But more often than not, from what I've seen, if there's even a little bit of clutter in the family room and a few dirty dishes by the sink, the whole beautiful effect of the home is ruined. The house just looks messy.

If your entryway offers a view into too many rooms in your home, you might try establishing various concealers to redirect the view. Life is messy sometimes, especially when it's creative or delicious or fun, so don't let a poorly conceived sight zone hinder your family's activities.

The most effective concealing is done by architectural changes, such as building a wall or putting doors on previously open doorways. If you implement architectural changes, make sure the resulting welcome area is nicely decorated and doesn't seemed cramped. You also don't want to block the flow of your home, but limiting your sight zone can greatly reduce your housekeeping stress and increase your home's positive first impression.

If architectural changes are too extreme, consider creating a temporary concealer by using:

- a big piece of furniture in the sight line, turning it in such a way that it doesn't block the flow but directs the view away from certain areas of the house

- an angled mirror, which will also make the entry space look larger

- a folding screen

- plants, perhaps on a tall plant stand or hanging from the ceiling

- a beautiful curtain

- a trellis

Your creativity is limited only by the design of your home, your budget, and what sort of space your welcome area includes.

Corral Your Necessary Messes

Every home has those areas that may appear cluttered to an outsider but in fact are necessary and functional, such as the family bulletin board or the front door launching pad. A House That Cleans Itself can have these things too, but they will be placed in such a way that they can be hidden at a moment's notice, instantly turning an area that looks messy into one that is neat.

Take, for example, the problem identified in step 1:

> *Magnets and papers cluttering up front of fridge.*

The reason those things are there is because:

> *Those papers are important reminders and have to go somewhere so we can see them on a regular basis*

The root cause, then, is:

> *We need a better place to put important papers where we'll notice them but they won't look so messy.*

If you're willing to be clever and resourceful, this may not be as difficult as you think. Perhaps you could mount some cork board on the inside of a well-placed cabinet door or two. If you choose doors that can stay open without causing any inconvenience, then leave them that way most of the time so that your important papers remain in full view. But if you want to neaten up in a hurry, all you have to do to corral that necessary mess is close those cabinet doors and the area is instantly clean.

If you have no doors that will suffice, consider hanging a bulletin board with a curtain or shade mounted above. You'll need to choose the area carefully lest this end up looking odd, but I've seen it done well, and with the flick of a pair of curtains, a huge mess disappears in an instant.

Utilize Camouflage

The third method for creating a first impression of clean is to utilize the power of camouflage wherever possible. We're all aware of this technique in our housekeeping efforts whether we realize it or not. That rug that never seems to show dirt? That countertop that always looks clean—until you touch it and realize it has crumbs on it? These things *seem* clean because their design easily camouflages dirt and mess.

I'm a big fan of camouflage. From permanent fixtures, such as linoleum patterns or carpet colors to more temporary items, such as bedding choices and appliance finishes, resolve to make an item's ability to camouflage dirt and stains a priority whenever making decisions about what to bring into your home.

If you have pets, remember to camouflage with them in mind. For example don't get dark carpeting if your dog is white and vice versa. Ditto for that new couch.

Do you live in a region where the dirt is known for its reddish clay tint? Then make sure all welcome mats and runners have a reddish tint in their design as well.

Does the outside of your car always look dirty? Believe it or not, the best car colors for hiding dirt and dust are the light ones, such as silver, champagne, and even white. The colors that show dirt the most are dark, such as black and dark blue.

Though few of us can afford to go out and purchase all new furniture, flooring, countertops, and more just for the sake of hiding our dirt, always keep this principle of camouflage in mind when shopping for something new.

Eliminate Inevitable Invisibles

Inevitable invisibles are what I call those things that contribute to an overall feeling of disorder or disrepair—stains, tears, rust, frayed edges, and nicks—but that you rarely notice because you've been living with them so long they have become invisible to you.

As you went through step 1 of the HTCI System, I hope you discovered many of these issues thanks your altered perspectives of height (on the step stool) and photos. Now that you've come to step 3, it's time to go ahead and deal with these problems, making whatever changes you can to improve the overall feeling of clean. For example, you may need to:

+ touch up chipped paint

+ replace shabby or worn items

+ remove stubborn stains

+ reapply discolored grout

+ replace rusty hardware

+ have a rug professionally cleaned

+ run your curtains through the wash

+ go to town with some elbow grease and effective cleaning tools

My friend Abby tells how she wasted valuable minutes every time she cleaned by trying to polish the brass switch plate beside her front door, to no avail. It always looked dull and marred. Killing time in a home repair center one day while waiting for her husband, she spotted an array of switch plates for sale. Much to her surprise, she realized she could replace the problem switch plate for a shiny new one for about ten dollars. Considering the amount of time she'd wasted trying to clean something that was never going to get clean, she felt silly. It never crossed her mind that the item could be replaced so cheaply or easily.

We lived for several years with a faucet that looked dirty and gunky all the time no matter what I did to clean it. I couldn't understand what I was doing wrong until my plumber was there one time working on a sluggish drain and happened to mention how sloppily the sink's faucet had been caulked. Sure enough, I had been spending my time on something that was *never* going to get any cleaner. Once I got it fixed, the whole sink area looked nicer for it.

This step of eliminating inevitable invisibles can involve some fairly labor-intensive tasks such as painting, repairing, scrubbing, and more. As you work, just remember that the effort you put in now can make a world of difference in maintaining a House That Cleans Itself for a long, long time to come.

I saw this principle in action in the home of a friend, who was wasting an enormous amount of time and effort trying to get her dingy kitchen floor clean the conventional way. Because she is housekeeping impaired, I think she figured that somehow if she just mopped harder or found the right brand of cleaner or wanted it badly enough that her grimy-looking white-tile kitchen floor would magically get clean. Unfortunately, that wasn't going to happen. The stains were too strong, too old, and too ground in. I suggested she put the mop aside and deal with the problem head-on. The only way she was going to eliminate that ground-in dirt was by getting down on her hands and knees and scrubbing the tiles with a Magic Eraser.

It wasn't easy or fun—but it was miraculous. After one prolonged scrubbing session, her floor looked great, and her whole cleaning routine was drastically shortened. Now all she has to do to keep her kitchen floor looking that way is give it a quick, occasional pass with a Swiffer WetJet or something similar. That's it. Because she dealt with the nastiness and got rid of it once and for all, her efforts at hard cleaning resulted in a floor that now needs only light cleaning.

The truth is, converting your home to a House That Cleans Itself can be a lot of work and occasionally even require elbow grease and special tools, but once that work has been done, the hard part is over. Between the relaxing feel of a clean-looking house and the time saved keeping it that way, the effort more than pays off.

As you go about arranging, improving, and organizing your home, always do it in such a way that it gives out that elusive feeling of clean to all who enter there, regardless of whether you've actually done any cleaning lately or not. By controlling your sight zones, corralling your necessary messes, utilizing camouflage wherever possible, and eliminating those inevitable invisibles where you can, you'll be well on your way to achieving a House That Cleans Itself.

My Most Embarrassing Messy House Story
—A Bathroom Surprise—
BY LINDA P.

When I was first married, I thought my new husband would clean up after himself the way my dad did, so I helpfully put cleaning supplies in the bathroom next to the mudroom where he kept his farm clothes. I rarely if ever looked in that bathroom, assuming he was taking care of it.

One fall day, about a week after they had been planting wheat on the farm, I peeked in there and saw something odd. I ventured in to take a closer look and realized that seed wheat must have fallen out of my husband's coveralls, landed on the warm, wet bath mat, and germinated. By the time I discovered it, there was wheat almost four inches high growing from the bath mat!

7

Think like a Hotel

STEP 4

*My son, do not let wisdom and understanding out of
your sight, preserve sound judgment and discretion;
they will be life for you, an ornament to grace your neck.
Then you will go on your way in safety, and your foot
will not stumble. When you lie down, you will not be
afraid; when you lie down, your sleep will be sweet.*

PROVERBS 3:21-24

This step takes its cue from the hospitality industry. Because so much of a hotel's operating costs are for housekeeping labor, numerous ways have been found to streamline the cleaning process as much as possible.

Fortunately, you can adapt many of these techniques for your home as well, shaving hours off of your cleaning routines and eliminating mess before it starts. These techniques include:

+ choosing fixtures, furnishings, and other possessions based in part on how easy they are to clean
+ arranging furniture in more cleaning-accessible ways
+ following the "up and away" principle
+ utilizing the power of beauty

- making fixes that do the work for you
- creating stations

Choose Fixtures, Furnishings, and Other Possessions Based in Part on How Easy They Are to Clean

This may sound like pat advice, but stick with me here. In a hotel, choices in carpets, lighting fixtures, bedspreads, and so forth are made not just with an eye toward design and comfort but also ease of cleaning. For example:

- hotel carpets usually have looped pile rather than cut, which is far more durable, and usually feature speckled tones and subtle patterns that camouflage well
- walls are usually papered rather than painted so fingerprints won't show
- table surfaces are sturdy enough to resist water rings and the nicks and scratches of daily wear and tear
- linens and towels are monochromatic for ease in laundering and stain removal

Even though few of us could afford to replace such items in our homes as part of converting to a House That Cleans Itself, these are principles to keep in mind whenever purchasing anything new. I even apply this idea to clothing and have a strict policy of never buying anything that has to be dry-cleaned. This not only saves me time and money, but I have eliminated that messy "Take to the dry cleaner" pile that used to gather and sit by the door for far too long.

Arrange Furniture in Convenient, Cleaning-Accessible Ways

This one's a bit of a no-brainer, but that doesn't mean it has occurred to the average housekeeping-impaired person. In a House That Cleans Itself, furniture placement is never an impediment to cleaning.

Think of a hotel room and how the beds are almost always arranged: with three sides accessible. Why? To make it as easy as possible to change the linens.

Do you have beds up against the walls long ways in your home? Do yourself a favor and turn them out from the wall the regular way. Is heavy furniture placed so close together that the vacuum cleaner can't pass through? Do some shifting, with the vacuum nearby, and then test it out to make sure you've given yourself enough room.

Remember, the goal, as always, is to engineer cleaning convenience. And hotels are experts on that.

Follow the "Up and Away" Principle

Hotels frequently use what I call the "up and away" principle, where many items are mounted on the wall—lamps, tissue dispensers, blow driers—rather than left to sit on horizontal surfaces. I used to think this was to prevent theft, but then I learned the main reason: The fewer items that have to be moved out of the way at cleaning time, the easier and faster it is to wipe and dust.

This is a great technique to borrow for your home, and one that has an immediate payoff. Over the years, I've gone "up and away" with almost everything I can, drastically reducing the cleaning time in almost every room of my house. As a bonus, I have found that this also helps eliminate a feeling of clutter.

Think about it. What can you mount in your home?

+ Lamps
+ Tissue dispensers
+ Blow driers
+ Toothbrush holders
+ Telephones
+ Televisions
+ Clocks

- ✦ Magazine holders
- ✦ Wine racks
- ✦ Mug racks
- ✦ Makeup mirrors
- ✦ Fans
- ✦ Coatracks
- ✦ Vases
- ✦ File folder holders
- ✦ Can openers
- ✦ DVD players

Think "up and away" in your home and drastically cut your cleaning time.

Utilize the Power of Beauty

Did you know that the more aesthetically pleasing a room is, the more likely it is to remain clean? I'd always heard this as a rule of thumb but never gave it much thought until I saw it happening in front of my own eyes—right after we renovated our kitchen.

Prior to the renovation, the kitchen was a near-constant mess. No matter how often I nagged my family, there were always sticky spots on the worn floor, crumbs on the scratched counters, and fingerprints on the ugly cabinets.

Once we gutted the room, however, and turned it into something far more lovely, the most miraculous thing happened: Nobody wanted to mess it up. Spills on the floor got wiped up immediately. Crumbs and fingerprints didn't stand a chance. My kids even started putting their dirty plates into the dishwasher without being reminded! We were motivated by the beauty of the room to keep it looking fabulous at all times.

Never underestimate the value of gorgeous when it comes to keeping a place clean. Beauty motivates when nothing else will. That doesn't mean you have to do a complete renovation. It is just a reminder that attractive spaces are more likely to stay clean than unattractive ones. It's also a pretty good excuse to get moving on that redecorating project you've been thinking about for a while.

Make Fixes That Do the Work for You

The next time you're at a hotel, pause for a moment near the entrance and take a look at the elaborate system they have set up for getting dirt off of your shoes as you come inside. Chances are good that there won't just be a simple industrial mat inside and out like you'll find at most businesses, but instead they'll have huge, elongated, roughly textured supermats that start well before the door, extend through the entryway, and continue partly into the lobby.

This is because they know that the more thoroughly the bottom of your shoes can be scrubbed off on the way in, the less work they will have to do to keep the place clean. This is the kind of fix that does the work for you, a technique you should employ throughout your home.

And even though you might not choose to sport 15 feet of rubber matting at your front door, you should definitely have the roughest, strongest mats you can find outside every entrance to your house, with a second mat inside each of those entrances. Following this simple rule will go a long way toward reducing the time you spend vacuuming and mopping.

Other fixes that do the work for you include the following:

Water treatment. Talk to your plumber or local water utility about whether there's a need for installing a water treatment system in your home. If you have unusually hard water, for example, a softener can decrease the staining in your tubs and sinks. (It will also increase the life of your washing machine.)

Air filters. Change the filter on your central air conditioner regularly. A clean filter can prevent the spread of dust and improve the air quality in your home.

Upgrades. The next time you upgrade your windows or doors, check the latest low-maintenance features on the market. Two of my favorites include blinds encased inside the glass (no more dusting mini blinds!) and top-hung sliding glass doors so dirt doesn't collect in a track below. Even lower-cost windows are now coming standard with easy-to-clean features such as a tilt-in capability.

Self-cleaning options. Whenever you do any home improvements, check to see if there are self-cleaning versions available for the products you need. Self-cleaning glass, for example, is a miracle of nanotechnology that will save you time all over your house. Self-cleaning glass is coated in titanium dioxide, which works with the sun and the rain to do the cleaning for you. The sun's ultraviolet light reacts with titanium dioxide to break down the organic chemicals in dirt, and then the rain produces a sheeting action that washes away the larger particles. There are also self-cleaning house paints, wood varnishes, and more with new products and improvements coming out all the time.

Painting. When painting a damp area, such as a bathroom or basement, consider using a mildew-resistant paint additive. This is usually sold in a packet at the paint store and can be added to almost any kind of paint by the technician during the coloring process.

Removing mud. If you live in an especially muddy area, or if the people in your home work in jobs or play sports that tend to cake mud on their shoes, consider installing an old-fashioned boot scraper outside your main entryway.

Floor mats. Though this change won't exactly do the work for you, it will help you feel better as you do the work: Put antifatigue mats in front of your sink or stove or wherever else you spend a lot of time standing as you perform household tasks. Good mats aren't cheap, but the moment you bring one home and put it in place, you'll understand why it's worth every penny. It will save your back, knees, hips, and more, especially if you have hard-surface floors such as ceramic tile.

Trash cans. One of the most effective changes you can make throughout your home is to ensure that there is a trash can in every single room and that the cans in the primary areas of trash accumulation—the kitchen, bathrooms, and home office areas—are large enough to handle the job. This may sound obvious, but to the housekeeping impaired, adequate means of trash disposal can be a bit of a blind spot. Not only do we provide too few cans, we often make them too small and too inconveniently placed. For the housekeeping impaired, throwing away trash should always require a single motion—which rules out cans in cabinets, cans with lids, cans that require any sort of extra steps to use. By making it easy to throw away trash throughout your home, you'll be amazed at the ways clutter and mess almost magically disappear.

Create Stations

The final way to think like a hotel is to create stations throughout your home. A station is simply a collection of items you store together because they will be used together.

Think, for example, of the coffeemaker in the average hotel room. It's usually on a tray, along with packets of coffee, sweeteners, stirring sticks, mugs, and everything else you'll need to make a cup of coffee. This is a station, and because all of these items are stored together in one place, the process of making a cup of coffee has been streamlined.

The opposite of a station is a rabbit trail. If you are housekeeping impaired, you're probably quite familiar with rabbit trails. These are the journeys you go on daily as you try to accomplish the various tasks of life. Whether it's getting the lunch money ready to send to school, wrapping a gift, or mailing a package, sometimes you have to wander through several rooms—or even the whole house—to gather your supplies. That gathering takes time and energy and serves to create mess, especially if you don't always put those items back where you found them.

In a House That Cleans Itself, all rabbit trails are identified and then eliminated by the establishment of stations. Whatever your rabbit trails, the key to eliminating them involves three steps:

1. All of the needed items for a given task are identified and collected.

2. The collection is placed in a single container in an appropriate storage area, such as a cabinet or drawer, in the room where you are most likely to perform the task.

3. Any of the collected items that might also be needed for performing other tasks in other locations, such as scissors, staplers, rolls of tape, etc., should be duplicated whenever you can afford it so that these items will be left alone and allowed to remain in their individual stations.

There are many common rabbit trails that may be eating up time and making a mess in your house. Any sort of task that sends you rooting around for its related tools at least once a month should be addressed.

For example, one of the most helpful stations in any home is the one for wrapping gifts. Your gift-wrapping station can be as simple or elaborate as you want. For years mine held only scissors, a roll of tape, and the Sunday comics. Nowadays, though I'm not a gift-wrap fanatic like some of my more artsy friends, I do take a pass on the comics in favor of pretty wrapping paper and curling ribbon or gift bags and tissue paper. The key is to put everything together in one place: gift wrap, tape, scissors (that are used only here and never carted off), labels or tags, and a permanent marker. In my house, I keep all of these items together in a single clear plastic bin, which stays in a storage area near the family room.

What I have to avoid—and you should too—is the temptation to hoard tiny scraps of wrapping paper in anticipation of wrapping a really small box. Paper scraps belong in the trash or recycle bin even if they are pretty. Also make a habit of tossing any wrapping paper that gets crushed or bent. If it's too raggedy to use on a gift, why hang on to it?

For examples of other common stations and the types of items that you may want to include in them, see chapter 13, "Sample Stations."

After you have created your stations, if you find the items are being carried off and not returned, don't hesitate to nip the problem in the bud, as follows:

+ Use a permanent marker to label the items by their station, just as people do in busy offices where fellow employees inadvertently take things from desks and never return them. For example, you might label one pair of scissors: "Gift-Wrapping Station. Do not remove!"

+ Have a talk with the thieves and establish penalties for misappropriation of station items.

+ Choose a less visible area for that station (for example, a bottom side drawer rather than a basket atop the desk so there is less temptation to pull from it.

+ Tie items down. After years of battling with my daughters, who were forever stealing my best hairbrush, I tied one end of a long string to the hairbrush and the other end to a dresser knob. It didn't look very pretty, and it was irritating to brush my hair that way, but over the next few weeks the string helped my girls become more aware of the fact they were grabbing the brush and walking away as they were using it. Once that lesson was firmly established and their habit broken, I removed the string.

Do whatever it takes to keep your stations intact. Embrace this concept, and you'll find that creating and maintaining stations saves you an enormous amount of time and energy all over the house.

Think like a hotel and have fun streamlining the cleaning process in your home.

My Most Embarrassing Messy House Story
—My Not-So-Secret Clutter—
BY BERNARD B.

In transition between apartments, I once rented a bedroom in the large home of a friend. With full kitchen and living room privileges,

I was careful to clean up after myself out there, particularly as the homeowner was a neat freak. I was much less careful in the bedroom I was using, where I tended to let things get out of hand.

One day I came home earlier than expected to find a crowd of neighbors hovering in the hallway outside my room, looking inside. The homeowner was with them, but when he spotted me, he looked guilty, as though he'd been caught red-handed.

"What's going on?" I asked.

When no one answered, the little girl from across the street piped up. "He's letting people come see how messy your room is. He does it all the time."

8

Aim for Simplicity

STEP 5

Sell your possessions and give to the poor.
Provide purses for yourselves that will not wear out,
treasure in heaven that will never fail,
where no thief comes near and no moth destroys.
For where your treasure is, there your heart will be also.

LUKE 12:33-34

From furniture choices to quantity of possessions, simplicity is always the goal in a House That Cleans Itself. The simplicity principle applies to your home in three ways:

1. Less stuff equals less mess, so eliminate the clutter.
2. Simple choices equal simple cleaning, so avoid ornate, highly detailed furnishings and other possessions whenever possible.
3. Keep it uniform to keep it clean. The fewer surfaces and finishes in your home, the fewer products and processes will be required to maintain them.

This chapter will explain each of these principles in turn.

Less Stuff Equals Less Mess

If you have trouble keeping your house clean, there's a very good chance that *you have too much stuff*. It's a cold, hard truth that no home can be consistently clean if it's overloaded with things. You probably know this already and have tried to clear out your clutter in the past without much success. That may be in part because all you've ever heard were the same old rules of thumb espoused by the experts. Those rules may work for the naturally gifted at housekeeping, but for those who are housekeeping impaired, we need a different way to deal with excess. Allow me to provide you with a new and unconventional method for facing this issue and clearing out the clutter once and for all.

According to the experts, there's a wide variety of reasons why we allow ourselves to hang on to too many items. Some of our most common justifications are:

+ I may need it someday.

+ I have a sentimental attachment to it.

+ It was given to me as a gift.

+ I inherited it.

+ I got a really good deal on it.

+ You never know when you might need two or three of these.

+ It holds the promise of fun or adventure.

+ I might be able to make something out of it.

+ It represents the life I'd like to be living.

+ I can get more for it if I hang on to it until I have time to sell it on eBay.

+ My children might want it someday.

+ Somebody else might need it.

Despite all of the above rationalizations, too much of a good thing is still too much. If you really want a House That Cleans Itself, you must start looking at your home with a more discerning eye. Remember how it appeared from atop your step stool? A room filled with unnecessary items can never be consistently clean. How can it be if there's simply too much there to contain?

As you think about separating the wheat from the chaff in your home, it's important to note that clutterers tend to fall along a spectrum. At one end of this spectrum is the person who may hang onto a wayward item or two out of forgetfulness or habit but who has no problem getting rid of such things as soon as they realize what they have done.

In the middle of this spectrum are what we usually call "pack rats," those people who tend to hang on to way too much stuff for a variety of reasons. Their cluttering problem springs from habit, personality style, lack of knowledge, lack of discipline, distractibility, or something else, but rarely is it based on any true *need* to clutter. If pack rats will focus on fixing the reasons they clutter in the first place, they can be quite successful in changing their ways. And although they will always struggle somewhat with this issue, by setting up specific routines, habits, and strategies, pack rats can learn to live with this problem and keep it from getting the best of them in the future.

At the far end of the spectrum are "hoarders." Hoarding is defined by the specific behaviors of acquiring too much and discarding too little (even items most people would consider useless). Consequently, they create such clutter-filled living spaces that those spaces cannot be used for their intended purposes.

Like pack rats, hoarders hang on to clutter for a variety of reasons. The difference is that they have a deep-rooted *need* to keep things and a strong resistance to letting go. Many hoarders call themselves "pack rats," but in truth their situation is much more dire. Letting go of their stuff creates deep anxiety within them, causing a vicious cycle of acquiring, clinging, and denial. If you've ever attempted to help a hoarder loosen their grip on their possessions, you know how strong that grip can be. If you love someone who is a hoarder, or you suspect you are a hoarder yourself, I strongly urge you to seek help for this problem. It is rooted in physiological and psychological issues that *can* be treated successfully. For more information, see chapter 18, "Mind over Matter."

Too Much Stuff

Wherever you fall on the above spectrum, if you have a problem with clutter, chances are you have spent a lifetime hearing different methods for clearing away your stuff. Most experts suggest asking yourself several key questions, such as "Do I really need this?" and "Have I used it in the last year?"

I say that if you were capable of answering those sorts of questions, the clutter never would have built up in the first place. You don't need better answers. You need better questions.

If you really want to get rid of clutter, in my opinion the place to start is in understanding and embracing this single truth:

> *Every possession you have, from the tiniest button to the biggest*
> *piece of furniture, consumes a piece of your time.*

Think about it. You spend time on your stuff when you acquire it, when you clean it, when you move it, when you shove it into a box and put it into the basement, when you kick it out of the way because you stepped on it, when you leave it out and the kids mess with it, when you get it dirty and have to wash it, when you fish it out from under the bed, when you hold it in your hand and try to decide what to do with it, when you sort it again, when you store it again, when you decorate with it, when you think about how much you love it, when you feel guilty about how much it cost, when you try it on and it no longer fits, when you dust it...and so on. Think of something completely insubstantial in your home, such as a safety pin or an emery board. If you have ever interacted with that item, you have spent time on it merely because it is one of your possessions.

The questions to ask yourself about your stuff as you attempt to weed things out are not value judgments about when you used it last or when you might need it again. To clutterers, there are too many shades of gray in those questions. Instead, face the black-and-white reality of the true trade-off you're making. When you are de-cluttering, with every single item you own ask yourself these questions:

- ✦ Is this item worth my time?

- ✦ Does what I get from this item provide a fair trade-off considering the time I'll have to spend cleaning and storing it?

- ✦ Do I want to spend another second in the future fooling with it, or do I want to get rid of it now so it will no longer cost me a single moment of time?

Probably both the safety pin and the emery board are worth keeping. When you pop a button at the last minute or have a broken nail, your time investment in those items pays off.

But what about that cute little wicker basket you've never quite figured out what to do with? What about that glass vase that came with a bouquet of flowers but you've never used it again because you already have better, prettier vases? Those 4 spatulas, 7 hot pad holders, 16 flashlights, and 22 pillowcases? Those remote controls that stuck around even after the equipment they came with went to the electric recycling center? Those obsolete computer parts? Those old phone wires, cable TV connectors, and frayed extension cords? Is that pile of mail-order catalogs worth one more minute of your time?

What do you own that's only worth the few seconds it will take to throw it away or give it away and stop it from using up another fraction of your life?

Consider the constant lament of the housekeeping impaired when de-cluttering, the "What if I need it someday?" syndrome. Okay, what if you do? What if that thing really will make a cute turtle costume three or five or seven years from now? I'm not telling you to get rid of it. I am saying, do the math. Which would take less time, hanging on to it and continuing to store it, move it out of the way and clean it so that you'll have it once you're ready for it, or toss it now and get another one down the road if and when the need really does arise? You see, if that thing you're reluctant to toss is inexpensive and easy to replace, and there's a good chance you may never need it anyway, then you would be wasteful to hang on to the one you have. Ditch it! Is it really worth *one more minute* of your time? If it turns out you did need it after all, you can always get a new one. On the other hand, if the item is unique and irreplaceable or extremely valuable, then you may be justified in hanging on to the one you already have. Only you know what's worth keeping and what isn't. But if you make such decisions based on the total time investment that item will require, it's far easier to see where those decisions should fall.

Stuff has a trade-off, and that trade-off is time. One spatula is worth the time it takes to clean it and store it because it's paying you back in return through its usefulness. But four spatulas? Now your time cost has gone up because not only do you have to clean them and store them, but you also have to spend time finding them (rustling through an overloaded kitchen tool drawer), making room for them (why won't this drawer close?), choosing between them (I use this one for pancakes but that one for hamburger patties), and maintaining them (this plastic handle feels as though it might be coming loose).

At what point does the weight of that trade-off fall to the wrong side? Only you know the answer to that question, but when you can admit that *stuff* eats *time*, it's easier to make the hard decisions that allow you to release your grip on things. In this world, there are many inequalities, such as income, opportunities, or education, but time is the great equalizer. Until we die, we all have 24 hours every day.

Do you really want to keep wasting your hours on *stuff*?

Removing the Clutter from Your Home

Once you understand the above concept, it's time to start purging excess throughout your home. But before you open a closet or prepare a single box or bin for Goodwill, there's an important first step you need to take: You need to figure out exactly what you are going to do with the items you will be weeding out of your home.

That means doing a little information gathering, making note of what you learn, and then using that information as you begin to clear out your stuff. The reason this step is first and not last is because this is the one that usually trips up the housekeeping impaired. We can pull out a stack of old and unwanted clothes, no problem. For us, the hard part is getting them out of the house and over to someplace that needs them. Even with the best of intentions, we're not all that great at the follow-through when it comes to donating our unwanted stuff.

Thus, if you want to donate items to a thrift store or charity, or if you want to sell it through a consignment shop, before you even start going through your things, gather the info you're going to need. Call to find out if they will pick up your things at your house and what you're supposed to do when you're ready to schedule that. If they don't offer that service, ask what the days and times are for taking your stuff to them. Ask also what items they do and do not accept, and if they have any special rules, particularly with regard to how you package everything. (For example, one place near us accepts boxes but not bags.) You may end up donating to several charities, especially if you have items that some places will take and others won't. Keep the telephone numbers and information handy so that when you're ready with your stuff you can get it out of your house right away. In case you find it helpful, I have included Donation Charts for recording this information in part 4 of this book.

While you're at it, get a copy of your town's guidelines for hazardous waste disposal as well. (Check online or at your local township building or library, or call your trash disposal company.) Once you have these guidelines, post them in your recycling area or laundry room. That way, when you have a burned-out fluorescent lightbulb or run across an old motherboard, you won't be tempted to set it aside to deal with later and allow it to create more clutter. Instead, you can consult the list and find out exactly how and when such items can be gotten rid of for good.

Once you've gathered all of the above information, there's one last thing to do before you start: Choose a temporary (*very* temporary) storage place for the items you'll be getting rid of. For the donated loads you'll be delivering yourself, consider using the trunk of your car. When you fill a bag or box, take it to the trunk and put it in, and then every time your trunk is full, make a run to the donation site. For some reason, we housekeeping impaired often think we have to wait until we have collected some huge amount of stuff and then bring it all in at once. Not true. Even a single, small box or bag is perfectly appropriate and appreciated. The key is to get stuff out of your home, not build up some giant pile and then drop off everything in one fell swoop.

If you are planning a yard sale, make sure that you give yourself two important boundaries: 1) a time limit to hold the sale, beyond which the stuff gets donated, and 2) a promise that whatever doesn't sell on that day goes to charity *that day* or goes directly into the trash *that day*. After all you've gone through to extract these items from your home, the last thing you need is for them to work their way back in. If you think you might be tempted to hang on to some of the leftovers, then make arrangements for someone else to handle that part of the job and simply drive away the moment the sale is done. While you're off splurging some of your earnings on an ice cream cone, they can deal with carting away whatever items didn't sell.

For more helpful tips on effective yard sales for the housekeeping impaired, see the handy guide in part 4, "Having a Yard Sale the HTCI Way."

Special Incentives

As you clear out clutter, if you have trouble letting things go, one handy trick is to seek out added motivation. When I was doing my big de-cluttering, the Lord gave me a very special incentive: Just as I was starting to work my way through the kitchen and pull all of those extra pots and pans and dishes and small appliances I rarely used, I learned through my church of a woman on a limited income who was going to be moving into her own apartment after years of living with her daughter. She had nothing for her new kitchen and no resources with which to buy anything. I arranged for all of my excess to go to her. As I went through my things and eliminated clutter, I found the job much easier and more rewarding because I knew someone who would benefit from every single thing I was giving away. It was fun—and having a known recipient led me to pull out far more items than I would have without one.

When you start to de-clutter, if you're having trouble lettings things go, ask God to make the recipients of your donations more tangible to you. Is there a battered women's shelter in your town? A halfway house or rehab facility? Call and see if some of their residents could use some clothes or toys or household items. You might also contact the leader of a local Celebrate Recovery or other addiction support group to see if any of the members are starting over and could use stuff to set up their households. Local charities are usually so tightly networked that a single phone call will almost always lead you to the right person at the right place. We live in such an affluent society that it's easy to forget people are in need, real need, all around us. Recognizing that need and supplying it faithfully does wonders for loosening even the tightest grip.

Finally, if you just can't seem to let enough of your stuff go, use what I call the "Maybe System." Put everything you know you *ought* to get rid of but just can't into cardboard boxes labeled "Maybe." Then stash the boxes somewhere out of the way, such as in the attic. On your calendar, pick a date in six months (or even a year if that feels safer to you) and make a note to "Get Maybe boxes out of attic." When that date rolls around, it's final decision time. Perhaps during the weeks or months that have passed you've seen you don't need what's in the boxes. More importantly, you will have found that having a House That Cleans Itself is so wonderful you're not willing to let old clutter come back in. If that's the case, take one quick peek inside the boxes and then send them on their way. For some people, it's just easier to let go in stages rather than all at once.

Even if you're not ready for a house-wide de-cluttering, there are several specific types of focused de-cluttering—or "releases"—you may find helpful, such as a lifestyle release, a technology release, and a duplication release. An explanation and examples of these releases and more can be found in chapter 14, "Releasing Your Grip."

Simple Choices Equal Simple Cleaning

Before I created the HTCI System, I never thought twice about cleaning when I went shopping for my home. I judged potential purchases by whether they worked with my decor, if they were comfortable, or if they fit my budget, but never once did it cross my mind to also take into account how complicated they would be to keep clean.

But then one day an offhand comment by my housekeeper sent my mind reeling. We were in the midst of preparing for our kitchen renovation, and she just happened to be there the day my husband and I were leaving for the store to pick out our cabinets.

"Whatever you do, don't go with wainscoting!" she called as we headed out the door.

I stepped back inside to ask what she meant. One of the styles I was considering had wainscoting as part of the design.

"It's all about grooves and ridges. The more grooves and ridges your cabinet doors have, the harder they are to keep clean."

Wow, was that exchange an eye-opener for me—and it came just in the nick of time. Not only did we choose a cabinet style with minimal grooves and ridges, but that one choice proved so time-saving and helpful that I have applied this clean-smart way of thinking to almost every household purchase since.

Remember: Simple choices equal simple cleaning, so avoid ornate, highly detailed furnishings and other possessions whenever possible. They may be lovely, but the time and trouble they will suck from your life—time spent *cleaning* rather than *living*—just aren't worth it in the end.

Uniformity Equals Ease of Cleaning

Along these same lines, remember that uniformity of surfaces goes a long way toward ease of cleaning. In practical terms that means if you're choosing a new coffee table, go with the one that's all wood rather than the one that's a combination of wood and glass. Why? Because two surfaces means two cleaners, one for wood and one for glass. Worse, glass cleaner is tough on wood, and wood cleaner smears glass, so that means you have to go to even more trouble when cleaning it to make sure there's no crossover. Think of the time you could have saved by choosing an equally attractive alternative made with one surface rather than two.

Remember: The fewer surfaces and finishes in your home, the fewer products and processes will be required to keep them clean.

Without a doubt, simplicity is and always will be a struggle for the housekeeping impaired. We embrace it in theory but seem to have particular difficulty putting it into practice. By using these guidelines for de-cluttering and acquiring, you'll give simplicity a real chance to take hold in your home. That's a wonderful feeling—and one more step toward having a House That Cleans Itself.

My Most Embarrassing Messy House Story
—Vacation from Cleaning—
BY JUSTINE M.

Our friends used to loan us their vacation house in the mountains. We'd go there often for long weekends with our two small children. About halfway through one such weekend, I was getting tired of waiting on everyone hand and foot, so I declared a strike. After all, it was *my* vacation too! Soon the sink was piled high with dirty dishes, toys and clothes were strewn everywhere, and the entire house was a mess from one end to the other.

On our last night there we decided to go out to eat, get a good night's sleep, and attack the mess first thing in the morning. We would be leaving the next day anyway, so one more night of mess wasn't going to hurt anything...or so we thought.

Unfortunately, there was a slight mix-up about our timing. Thinking we had left that afternoon, the owners decided to start their own vacation a few days early.

They arrived while we were at the restaurant, and when we got back to the house, their car was parked outside. I nearly died. It would have been one thing to let my own house go, but it was quite another to do it to someone else's—and then have them see it that way before we were able to clean it back up!

They were incredibly gracious about it and never seemed to doubt that we would restore the home to its former pristine condition, which of course we did right then and as quickly as possible. But I've never gotten over the shame of being caught in such a mess.

9

Explore the "Why"

STEP 6

Search me, God, and know my heart;
test me and know my anxious thoughts.

PSALM 139:23

If you or someone in your home is housekeeping impaired, there may be reasons you have trouble keeping things clean that have nothing to do with the house at all. One of the most important steps to a House That Cleans Itself is to grasp various facts about the way your brain works and how that may be contributing to the problem. The good news is that often simply by understanding these uniquenesses, you can find clever ways to work around them. In other words, even when your house isn't part of the problem, it can still be part of the solution.

Following are descriptions of some common characteristics of the housekeeping impaired, provided in a helpful problem/solution format. As you work through this chapter, consider whether any—or all—of these characteristics apply to you or someone you love. If so, then you'll want to consider the work-arounds suggested so that these issues will no longer cause mess in your home.

Problem: You have a hard time remembering to pause, think, and do when it comes to the actions of daily life. Your brain is usually quite busy working on something unrelated to your body, so many of your physical actions are done without conscious thought. For example, when you're brushing your teeth, chances are you are also designing a living room, plotting a novel, or planting a garden—in your head, at least.

Because your brain is otherwise occupied most of the time, any physical action that also requires a moment of thought (such as picking up a wayward sock, straightening a towel on a rack, or putting away a jacket rather than tossing it on a chair) is not going to get done. Your body may be there in the house, but your brain is not. You tend to ignore or not notice any action that requires you to interrupt your thoughts. This is how you are hardwired. Are you a slob? Not at all. Unfortunately, to people who aren't this way you can come across as messy and even inconsiderate.

Solution: Here are three ways you can compensate for this type of impairment.

1. *Set up your home so that doing the neat thing is as mindless a process as doing the messy thing.* For example, replace the chair you usually dump your jacket on with a standing coatrack.

2. *Take a five-minute walk through your entire house once a day and focus on what's in front of you.* This is when you'll pick up those socks and straighten those towels. Set a timer if you have to, but on this walk do not do any heavy cleaning, just light straightening, and don't allow your mind to wander. As difficult as this may be in the beginning, if you do it daily, it can become a pain-free habit.

3. *Use labels everywhere so you don't have to think or remember when putting things away.* My family rolls their eyes at my labeled life that extends from the linen closet shelves to almost every shelf and bin in my office. But they don't have this mindlessness problem, so they don't understand that if I don't have labels to follow, I lose an enormous amount of time standing in front of a closet trying to bring my brain back into the moment, consciously realize what I'm holding in my hand, and then remember where I previously decided that item ought to go. Without labels, cleaning is so much trouble that I'm less likely to do it.

Problem: If you can't see it, you don't remember it. As it relates to clutter, this is a far bigger issue than most people realize. Do you tend to forget about something if it's not out and visible to you? Could that be one reason your house is a mess, because subconsciously you know if you put these things away you might never again find or even remember you have them? Maybe you don't have this problem so much with objects, but you do with papers. If your desk is covered with horizontal piles, I daresay this is an issue for you. Let a piece of paper go (or, worse, place it in a vertical file folder), and you know for a fact you will forget it ever existed.

Solution: If you are a "can't remember it if you can't see it" person, your main household goal must always be to set up systems that aren't just useful but are also visible. Think see-through: clear bins, clear containers, clear drawers. Once I committed to using only clear storage, it made a world of difference!

You also need to set up whatever memory-jogging helps you can throughout your house, such as bulletin boards, signs, labels, and reminders. Be sure to integrate them into your decor in such a way that they can easily be hidden or camouflaged when you want to tidy up.

Finally, you may need to forego vertical files almost entirely and find some other substitute for your papers. It's not easy to live a file-free life, but you can carry this idea much further than you might think by substituting horizontal sorters, boxes, and drawers.

Problem: When you organize, you tend to overdo by creating too many categories. Too many subdivisions make sorting complicated and challenging. Consider, for example, how you have organized your household papers. Even if you set up a good, simple sorting system by following someone else's guidelines, when it comes time to use it, you may find yourself standing there in confusion, item in hand, wondering what category that item is most closely related to. And even if you do manage to give it a home, later you can't remember which category you chose, forcing you to dig through all applicable file folders to find the missing paper.

If you don't know whether the receipt for your window unit air conditioner should be filed under major purchase receipts (it was $250), tax records (I'm using it in my home office), appliances (technically, is an air conditioner an appliance?), then this is an issue for you.

Solution: Think "broader is better" and force yourself to use more general categories. Whenever you set up any new system, from your spice cabinet to your linen closet to your DVD collection, always pause to ask yourself if you're carrying it too far. If you're not sure, ask someone else. His or her input will help you see if your organization is too extensive and may end up causing more problems than it will solve.

As for your papers, consider using boxes or drawers rather than files, and give them more general categories with more personalized headings. (For example, that air conditioner receipt could go into a box labeled "Papers Related to Stuff I Own.") This system may look inefficient to others, but for you this might be the answer to a lifetime of struggling with your tendency to overorganize.

You may also want to consider a digital database. Programs such as Paper Tiger are perfect for over-categorizers because they are designed to create a digital directory for a paper filing system. I'm not talking about scanning files or digitally filing the papers themselves. The only part of the process that's digital is the description of what is filed where. Each item filed is listed in the database by keyword, so when you need to find something later, all you have to do is type in one of the matching keywords and the program will tell you where to find the item you seek. In the above example, regardless of which folder you ended up choosing to put it in, all you would need to do to find it later would be to type in "major purchase" or "receipt" or "tax" or "appliance" and any one of those keywords would return a list of related filed papers and their locations, one of which would be "Receipt for window unit air conditioner—file no. 23 in drawer A."

Whether you're a database-type person or not, always remember, broader is better.

Problem: When you clean, you tend to get lost in the process, which costs you so much time that you aren't able to finish the job. It is a strange phenomenon that most people who consider themselves housekeeping impaired will flip to the opposite side of the spectrum once they get rolling. Before they know it, they are alphabetizing the entire CD collection or are on their hands and knees with a razor blade, scraping away gunk from along the base of the back door.

This is another big problem for me. I can't even remember how many times I set out to clean the whole house, top to bottom, and never made it past the second room. If you have trouble judging time—both estimating how much time something is going to take and how much time is passing when you're actually doing it—then that compounds the problem.

Solution: Try the following ideas to take care of this tendency.

1. *Always look at the big picture.* Take a quick inventory of a room first and force yourself to begin with the most important areas. For instance, in the kitchen, if dirty dishes are in the sink and newspapers are spread across the table, don't start by washing the windows.

2. *Clean with a portable timer.* Divide the number of minutes you have to spend by the number of areas you want to clean. The resulting number is how long to set the timer for each room. When the timer goes off, whether you are finished in there or not, move to the next room. Start the timer again. As long as you cooperate with the timer, this technique will keep you moving throughout the house.

3. *Clean with others.* Trade off with a friend. You give her two hours every Tuesday; she gives you two every Thursday. Or try what I call the Room-to-Room Sequencing method, described fully in chapter 21, "Cleaning a House That Cleans Itself." When I'm sequence cleaning, I know I have to stay on task because there are two people waiting for me to finish so they can get in there and do their jobs.

Problem: You are a perfectionist, or similarly, you are an all-or-nothing cleaner. You're not going to clean at all unless you can do it right and/or do it completely. The problem is that life doesn't often allow the luxury of that much uninterrupted time.

My mother tells the story of when she was newly married and eager to win a coveted "Good Housekeeping" certificate given once a year by the management of the apartment complex where she and my dad lived. On the day the contest judge arrived to inspect their apartment, it was spotlessly clean and not one thing was out of place. The judge was impressed, and it looked as though my mother was going to get the certificate she had worked so hard for...until the judge grabbed the edge of the gas stovetop and lifted it to reveal a greasy mess underneath. Never having had a gas stove before, and because the hinges were hidden, my mother didn't know the lid lifted or that grime could accumulate there. Despite all her hard work, she didn't qualify for the certificate.

The perfectionistic bent in Mom couldn't make her home perfect even though she did her best. She just didn't know everything...and, really, who does?

When I think of this story, I'm so glad it's not the 1950s anymore. I can't imagine someone coming into my home and judging my efforts. Even at its cleanest, my house would not win any prizes. Fighting this tendency toward perfectionism myself, I have spent a lot of time in the last few years changing my standards for what clean really looks like, which in the strange mathematics of perfectionism has actually resulted in a much cleaner house.

Are your standards so skewed that you would sacrifice *average daily cleanliness* for *perfect occasional cleanliness*? This all-or-nothing approach simply doesn't work in the day-to-day reality of life. Just as you can't lose weight if you eat like a king for six days and then fast on the seventh, you can't conquer your mess if you avoid all cleaning for six days and then go crazy cleaning from one end of your house to the other on the seventh.

Solution: To combat this problem, you have to see that it is a problem *and not just a personality quirk.* Perfectionists and all-or-nothingers can absolutely *paralyze* themselves by preferring complete inaction to doing something imperfectly or incompletely. Consequently, they miss out on a lot of life. They live amid mess much of the time. They avoid having people come to their homes except when their places are perfectly clean. If this sounds like you, I don't have any work-around tips to help you compensate. This one must be attacked head-on by refusing to allow these tendencies to have an effect on your cleaning behavior.

When I first realized this for myself, I had not yet converted my home to a House That Cleans Itself, so there was no consistency regarding the state of cleanliness. On any given day, the house might appear sparkling and spotless, dirty and disastrous, or somewhere in-between. When I saw that my perfectionist tendencies were contributing to this problem, I resolved to change. That change began with *raising my lowest standards* and *lowering my highest standards,* hoping they would more often meet in the middle. I also decided to stop going nuts trying to make the house perfect every time company was coming. This was hard for me, especially in the beginning, but I forced myself to have people over on a regular basis whether the house was spotlessly clean that day or not. A House That Cleans Itself is one that's *clean enough.* If you are housekeeping impaired, aiming for more than that is a recipe for disaster.

To help conquer my perfectionism, I came up with a saying: "They are not here to see a clean house, they are here to see us." I told myself this when friends stopped by for a quick hello and the breakfast dishes weren't in the dishwasher yet. I told myself this when my dad visited and we had to clear some piles from the spare bedroom to give him somewhere to sleep. But slowly, as I worked to conquer those tendencies, the strangest shift began to occur. Once the house didn't have to be perfect sometimes, it began to be okay more of the time. The cleanest days weren't so clean, true, but the messiest days weren't so messy either.

I knew I had sufficiently conquered my perfectionism the day I gave my daughters a surprise party. I invited all of the guests to hide in the dining room, even though I had run out of time before the party and hadn't been able to clear the table of several stacks of papers or vacuum the floor. (After the moment of surprise, the party was going to be relocated to the back deck, which had received preparty attention and was clean and nicely decorated.) Despite the fact that 15 people were crammed together in that less-than-perfect dining room, I realized they really weren't there to see a clean house. They were there for us, to celebrate with my older daughter, who was graduating from the eighth grade, and to celebrate with my younger daughter, who had just the week before been baptized. As I crouched on the rug that had some crumbs on it, listened to my husband usher the unsuspecting kids into the house, and held my breath in that final second before we all jumped up and yelled "Surprise!" I realized how far I had come. The way my house looked was no longer more important than the people who gathered in it.

This should be the goal of every perfectionist: to *not* need to be perfect. This should be the goal of every all-or-nothinger: to *not* have to finish everything. Ask God to begin to work such a change in you, as He has in me.

Problem: Through past problems and failures, you have developed aversions to many conventional tools and methods of organizing, such as putting papers into file folders. If you've spent a lifetime feeling stupid or guilty because conventional tools and methods don't work for you, it's time to stop beating yourself up.

Solution: Throw convention to the wind and base your solutions on the tools and methods that work for you. Give yourself the opportunity to try new solutions. Think outside the box! For example, I don't know why sliding papers into a slot doesn't appeal to me but dropping them into an open bin does. I have given up trying to figure out the "why" and instead decided to focus on the "what": what works for me in keeping this house clean, in helping me organize, in guiding me through the hours I am given in a day.

Ditch the "oughts," as in "you ought" to do something this way or that way. Says who? Do it in whatever way works for you. Just don't give up on finding ways to make it work.

Problem: In reaction to failed conventional methods, you feverishly acquire unconventional or complicated organizational devices, thinking they will finally solve all of your problems. Some unconventional devices can be very helpful, but many organizational tools actually suck up your time and in the end make more of a mess.

Terri thought she had finally found the perfect tool for handling, sorting, and using coupons. She mounted a "coupon handler bulletin board" in her laundry room that was divided vertically by category and horizontally by expiration date. For about a month she diligently placed her coupons in their appropriate squares, excited that she was finally going to take advantage of the great savings these coupons offered.

The problem was that whenever Terri went to the grocery store, she usually forgot to take the correct coupons. Even when she remembered them, once she got to the checkout line, she was so distracted with unloading, bagging, and paying that she would forget to pull them out of her purse and use them. Her enthusiasm dimmed, and at home she grew less diligent about sorting the coupons. Eventually she had a half-filled fancy bulletin board and four boxes of coupons to sort, most of which she was more than likely never going to use. Terri was frustrated.

Solution: Rather than beat yourself up about it a failed system, think about the lessons learned from that failure. Terri's conclusion was that she needed to give up the idea of using coupons entirely. For people with "out of sight, out of mind" issues, coupons cause more trouble than they're worth. She tossed out the coupons *and* the bulletin board and never let herself feel guilty about all those lost savings again. Instead, she focused on other ways to cut costs, such as joining a warehouse club and buying her veggies at a local produce stand.

When conventional *and* unconventional options fail, rather than racing around to find yet another tool, use what you've learned about yourself and your issues to come up with a better, simpler way of doing things. It's not about the tools; it's about your behavior and your brain. It's about figuring out what you *can* do to make cleaning and organizing feel less like a desperate swim upstream and more like a lazy paddle down the river.

Problem: When you decide to change, you jump in too far, too fast, and too enthusiastically…and burn out before you're done. Over the years the people who know me best have learned not to invest too heavily in some of my enthusiasms because they know most of them will peter out long before I establish true change or reach the end of a project. Is this true for you as well?

This is more than a personality issue. At its core, it's a spiritual issue. When we go running too quickly down a primrose path at full steam, we're running ahead of God—ahead of His timing and ahead of His blessing. Psalm 25:4-5 says, "Show me your ways, LORD, teach me your paths. Guide me in your truth and teach me, for you are God my Savior, and my hope is in you all day long." In our hurry we leave no room for learning or guidance. Our hope is not in God but in our own ideas and excitement. Psalm 46:10 says, "Be still, and know that I am God." How hard it is for some of us to be still! But that's exactly the character trait God yearns to develop in us.

Solution: Resist the urge to run off half-cocked every time you think you've found a new and better way to conquer mess. If God is in what you want to do, He will reveal that to you in His time. Resolve to stop entering into household purges and changes—even the ones described in this book—without first fully grasping the scope of what lies ahead. Whether you end up using the House That Cleans Itself System or something else entirely, make a commitment this time and stick with it to the very end.

Isaiah 40:29 reminds us that "[God] gives strength to the weary and increases the power of the weak." Rather than giving up when you grow weary, as you've done in the past, this time claim His promise that "those who hope in the LORD will renew their strength. They will soar on wings like eagles; they will run and not grow weary, they will walk and not be faint" (Isaiah 40:31). If you do find yourself feeling frustrated or exhausted, you need to relax, go slower, or take a break by choosing a smaller task you can conquer quickly.

Yes, it may take longer than you wish to purge your home of a lifetime of accumulations. Yes, it may get boring and frustrating sometimes to convert your house to a House That Cleans Itself. Yes, you may get tired. But no, you can't use your tiredness as an excuse to stop fixing this broken part of your life. When you reach the end of yourself, allow your weariness and loss of enthusiasm to send you straight into the arms of the One who wants to renew you. Be still. Listen to Him. Worship Him. Honor Him.

Then get back at it. Know this for sure: Eagles' wings are the very best housekeeping tool you'll ever find.

My Most Embarrassing Messy House Story
—Capturing the Moment—
BY CORINNE Z.

My child's birthday party brought much work—closets to clean, floors to scrub, clutter to hide. Hours later I had conquered it all. (I have a compulsion to clean everything if I'm going to clean anything.) The closets, gleaming and organized, brought tears of satisfaction to my eyes.

Until my father wandered in. According to him, the moment was so rare that he wanted to capture it on film. He ran back and got the video camera, and then he returned and began filming. In awe, he traveled from room to room, immortalizing the cleanliness on film—all the while quipping sarcastic commentary.

Sigh. At least he noticed it was clean.

10

Make It a Team Effort

STEP 7

Above all, love each other deeply,
because love covers over a multitude of sins.

1 PETER 4:8

No man (or woman, for that matter) is an island, so it's important to involve the whole family in turning your home into a House That Cleans Itself. This chapter will help you get everyone on board with this system—even a skeptical spouse, less-than-enthusiastic children, or any other naysayers who just happen to live with you—and then work together using a team approach as you employ creative problem solving throughout the house.

Rallying the Troops

You have two options for bringing others into your HTCI-inspired vision: Involve them from the get-go or start the ball rolling on your own in a few small ways and wait until they start to sense the positive changes around them before you reveal what you've been doing. Either method is fine. The one you choose should probably depend on your personality and that of your family members. The key is that when you present the basics of the plan, you do so in a pragmatic and upbeat manner. Stress the uniqueness of the HTCI System, the way it has been designed to work *with* your behaviors rather than against them, and how its primary goal is to keep your home "twice as neat in half the time."

When you put it that way, what's not to love?

Why It Matters

A clean home is serious business, yet when it comes to mess we often tend to make light of a subject that really isn't funny at all. Just talk to any adult who grew up amid excessive clutter or filth and it isn't hard to sense their pain. Chaos and disorder in a home can generate enormous sadness, anger, or anxiety. It can even lead to addiction as children learn to fill their craving for structure with other substitutes.

The opposite of disorder, on the other hand, can have tremendous benefits. Did you know that household order—characterized by routines and cleanliness—has been positively associated with early reading abilities?[1] That kids who are raised in clean homes are more likely to complete more school and have higher earning potential than those raised in dirty homes?[2] These facts don't surprise me. Children need to live where they aren't subjected to mess-related stress, where time is spent on learning and growing rather than rooting around trying to find stuff that's been misplaced or shuffling clutter from one haphazard pile to another.

Living in chaos also has a tremendous impact on our time. According to one study, the average American spends six minutes each morning looking for his or her car keys.[3] *Six minutes.* Add it up and that's an entire day and a half per year—just looking for our keys! Can you imagine what your total annual time investment is for the other minutes eaten up each day because of the clutter and chaos in your home? I shudder to think of the cumulative total I squandered in my messy past.

If your house is not consistently clean enough, you already know it's time to implement a real, working, practical, doable, functional solution to this problem—for your own sake and for the sake of your family. The HTCI System really can be the answer you've been looking for.

And while you can implement it on your own, if you can find a way to work together, there's no end to what your own personal HTCI Team can accomplish.

That All-Important Talk

Bringing your family on board with your plan starts with an earnest conversation between you and your spouse, if you have one. If housekeeping is an issue in your home, this will hardly be a new topic for the two of you. In fact, research shows that six of the top ten most frequent reasons married couples argue have to do with simple housekeeping issues.[4] (In case you're curious, these six offenses include nagging about chores, leaving hair in the drain, hoarding stuff, overfilling trash cans, leaving tissues around the house, and leaving dirty cups around the house.)

The same study showed that couples argue on average 312 times a year, which means we're all spending an awful lot of time sweating the small stuff. Chances are, if you can convince your spouse that you've found a workable solution for the messes in your home, he or she will be more than happy to implement that solution with you.

Common Objections

If you do meet with some objections, here are some of the more common ones you may hear, along with suggestions on how you might want to respond.

"This plan won't work." Arranging your house in a logical manner so that it more readily stays clean will always work. If this is your wife's objection, either do a better job of explaining how the system works or press further to find out what her real concern is here.

"I'm afraid you intend to spend a lot of money on this, money we don't have." If this is your husband's objection, assure him that the HTCI System can be implemented with little or no expense. Promise to make

only the no-cost or low-cost changes at first, and if you reach a point where you feel that an expenditure would greatly help the process, say that you'll discuss it at that time and decide then, together, whether it's worth it or not.

Remind him, too, how much money is wasted because of disorganization and mess. Have you ever added up late fees to the video store and the library? Discounts you didn't take advantage of because you responded too late? Coupons you cut out and never found again? Lost checks and cash? How about the cost of your time? Unless you're talking about hiring a butler, *living messy costs much more than living neatly,* especially if you have to bring in a weekly cleaning service just to stay on top of things.

"I'm afraid you'll put too many demands on me, and I'm overloaded already." If your wife says this, tell her that what you need primarily is her emotional support and cooperation, not her physical efforts. Let her know you respect her schedule and commitments and won't overload her. Remind her that in the long run, having a House That Cleans Itself will *lessen* everyone's burdens around the home and free up more time, sometimes quite significantly.

"Sorry, but we've been through this before too many times. I'm not about to get my hopes up again, only to see them dashed in the end." If this is the response you get from your husband, show some compassion and apologize for having let him down in the past. Assure him that he need not invest emotionally this time—at least not until he sees how well the plan is working. As long as he is willing to be a team player in front of the kids and not be an obstructionist, that's enough for now. For your own sanity, let the conversation end there. Don't waste time or energy trying to convince him how unique and logical the HTCI System is, or how it really can work for you where other systems have failed. Simply put the matter to rest, and then get to work and let your actions speak louder than your words for a change.

Working in Your Favor

If you still need help convincing a reluctant spouse, consider this interesting fact: Twenty-five percent of survey respondents acknowledged they had been more active and interested in cleaning their homes since the start of the recession. Apparently the troubled economy has prompted a need for empowerment, and the acts of cleaning, organizing, and de-cluttering a home can help fulfill that need.[5] If the recession has touched your family, you might bear this fact in mind and use it to help motivate your spouse.

Finally, if it's a stubborn hubby you're trying to bring on board, ask yourself:

Like most men, is he a born problem solver? Then he really can be a wonderful partner as you work your way through the HTCI System together. His innate ability to come up with logical solutions to even the most complex of challenges will give him—and your home—the chance to shine.

Like many men, is he utterly hopeless at finding things around the house? It's not just a myth. Per week, men spend an average of *one hour and twenty minutes* looking for the remote control, while women spend an average of *seven* minutes.[6] You might tactfully quote this statistic to your husband and point out to him that the more organized your home, the less time he'll waste on fruitless searches such as these.

Bringing the Kids in on It

Whether your spouse is 100 percent on board or not, it is important for the two of you to present a unified front to the children as you introduce the HTCI System to them. As with your spouse, the best way to do this may be to sit down for a heart-to-heart. Depending on your children's ages and maturity levels, you may want to start by asking them how they feel about the current mess, disorganization, division of chores, and so forth, in your home. Leave your defenses at the door—and be ready to hear some uncomfortable truths.

If they throw out terms like "frustrated" or "embarrassed," don't feel bad. In fact, be glad! You've got them right where you want them. Dissatisfaction with the status quo is a wonderful impetus for change. Explain to them that you've been frustrated with the house too, but that together all of you can turn the situation around and make your home into a House That Cleans Itself. Then communicate your enthusiasm for the plan in a way that helps them understand why this system will succeed where so many others have failed.

When Janey decided to implement the House That Cleans Itself System, she was surprised to meet opposition from her entire family. For the kids, they simply saw it as more chores. But as Janey described her goals, casting her vision of less mess, more free time, and less stress on everyone, they began to get on board.

If your children or teens are still objecting, it may be because they don't really understand how the system works or they fear it will mean more hassle for them. Let them express those thoughts. Then attempt to bring them around by answering their questions and addressing their concerns. Stress that while there may be some extra work at the beginning, the ultimate goal is far *less* work for everyone in the home, every single day.

Whatever you do, don't just announce the plan and then dictate how they should feel about it. Instead, present it in terms of their specific hopes, issues, and needs. For example, remind them of the field trip they had to miss because you lost the permission slip and didn't send it in. Tell them that by creating a House That Cleans Itself, you'll be able to keep better track of all of your papers so that nothing like that will ever happen again. Remind your preteen of how she felt when her friends came over to spend the night and saw that a bunch of her smelly, dirty clothes had made their way under the bed. Tell her that with a House That Cleans Itself, you might use a bit of clever problem solving and decide to block off the underside of her bed with wood slats so that she'll never be embarrassed that way again.

You shouldn't bring up past hurts to manipulate your children into doing what you want them to do, of course, but sometimes kids need reminding about obstacles from the past so they can see real, tangible value in your plans for the future. Done compassionately, this sort of conversation can be very effective.

Working as a Team Throughout the House

Once your whole family is on board, it's time for some group-friendly creative problem solving. This can be done in a variety of ways, but at the very least it means approaching your household messes collaboratively and coming up with solutions together. Having to work with others, especially kids, may sound tedious or unnecessary, but in fact the opposite is true. Bringing family members into the mix will:

+ encourage better brainstorming and help expand your list of possible solutions

+ give you new insight into what's causing various messes throughout your home

+ allow you to choose more workable, lasting solutions

+ give others "ownership" for those solutions, which in turn will help to guarantee success

Remember, a good sense of humor can go a long way toward keeping the peace as you solve the various messes around your home. Try to keep things light, perhaps even assigning nicknames to some of your worst habits.

For example, one term my husband and I coined years ago is "barnacling" in reference to the way barnacles will latch onto a ship's hull and stay there. In our house, barnacling is what we call the tendency to utilize any available horizontal surface by piling stuff on it that doesn't belong there. For some reason, the words, "Don't barnacle the coffee table," goes over a lot better than, "Get your stuff off the coffee table." The latter sounds like nagging while the former makes us both smile—and is a lot more effective in the long run.

Teamwork with Your Kids

Take, for example, the problem Lucinda had with her son, who wouldn't put away his equipment after playing video games. No matter how many times she reminded him, he almost always left the living room floor littered with his controllers, game discs, cases, and more.

The first step in solving a problem like this with a team approach would be to ask your child why he or she thinks it keeps happening. Sometimes children aren't being lazy or inconsiderate as much as they are avoidant for some undefined, subconscious reason. If you can broach the topic in a non-accusatory way and refuse to accept the pat response of, "Sorry, Mom. I'll try harder next time," the two of you just might be able to get past the frustration of the issue and come up with an actual root cause.

Is the storage area in an illogical place? Is it already too full or for some reason difficult to use? In Lucinda's case, what they finally figured out was that it was simply too high. Her son sat on the floor to play games, but the cabinet where his equipment was stored was at the top of the entertainment center and required him to stand up in order to use it. What was happening was that by the time he finished playing and stood, his mind had already shifted from what he'd just been doing to what he was about to go do next. He would head out of the room, oblivious to the fact that he'd forgotten to pick up all of his things and put them in that upper-level storage cabinet.

It sounds silly, but for those of us who are housekeeping impaired, these are the "lightbulb moments" that can change a house in surprising ways. All they had to do was switch around the cabinets so that the gaming equipment was stored down low. Once Lucinda's son could put his things away *while he was still sitting on the floor,* he was much more consistent in remembering to do so. And because he was the one who suggested that particular solution, he had a stake in proving that his idea was a good one.

Problem solved, thanks to facing it as a team. Had Lucinda tried to figure that one out on her own, she may never have connected the dots and come up with such a simple and logical resolution, one that actually worked more often than not.

Teamwork with Your Spouse

What if the issue isn't a messy child but a messy spouse? That can be a bit trickier, because for some reason our communal clutter tends to carry with it all sorts of emotional implications. Do you read more into your spouse's disorder than you should? Have you ever thought to yourself, *He does that because he knows it'll bug me,* or, *If she loved me, she'd clean that up*? If so, it sounds as though you may be falling into this common trap.

Of course, there are people in this world who tend to act out their emotions through their actions in this way, but unless your spouse is known to be passive-aggressive, chances are that's not what's happening in your home. The first ground rule for HTCI teamwork with your spouse, then, is to try to leave the emotion out of the process as much as possible—the negative emotion, that is. (Bring on the positives all you want, especially humor, affection, and lots of love.)

Let's say, for example, that your husband has the habit of leaving wet towels on the floor after his daily shower. There the towels will stay, damp and eventually stinky, unless you pick them up and carry them to the laundry room yourself. Perhaps in the past you saw this as a sign of disrespect for you, or at least an act of thoughtlessness. If you put those thoughts away, however, and look at the issue objectively, you may find that it is neither. It may in fact have a root cause that you've never thought to explore, much less solve.

To end this problem once and for all, start by asking your husband—without accusation or anger—why he thinks he has this habit. The answer may surprise you:

+ Maybe he's not really a towel rack kind of guy and some other sort of towel-hanging system would work better for him.

+ Perhaps the towel rack is too far away once he finishes
  with his towel each day, and he's in a hurry to get ready
  for work.

+ Perhaps a rack is nearby, but it's usually full of dry towels
  and he doesn't want to get them wet by placing his used
  one on top.

+ Perhaps he's been yelled at in the past for putting a towel
  back on the rack crooked, and he figures it's easier to
  throw his towel on the floor than to risk getting in
  trouble again for hanging it wrong.

Obviously, don't ask this question unless you're prepared to hear the
answer, but once the two of you have worked together to find the cause,
you can then work together to find the solution. Ask him what he thinks
it would take to keep the damp towels off of the floor from now on.

+ Perhaps he would find a hook on the back of the door
  appealing.

+ Perhaps he needs the convenience of a second towel rack
  in the bedroom rather than just in the bathroom.

+ Perhaps having a rack in the bathroom is fine, but
  he needs one that stays empty of other towels and is
  reserved for his use only.

+ Perhaps he just wants to be able to hang up his towel
  on the rack that's there without criticism from you for
  how it's hung, ever again. (If that's all he's asking, then
  I say dig deep and give him what he needs. There are far
  more important things in life than whether or not your
  beloved husband ever learns to properly hang up a towel.)

Whatever solution the two of you find, just remember that there's a
difference between an act that's thoughtless (leaving a mess for you to
clean) and one that's without thought (dropping a damp towel on the
floor because he's so focused on getting ready for work that he doesn't

even realize what he's doing). Thoughtless acts need emotional exploration, but acts without thought simply need creative problem solving.
Of course, not every such conflict can be solved so simply or amicably.
For navigating more complicated marital mess-related waters, see chapter 18, "Mind over Matter."

Once you've managed to solve this situation, just think: After years
of griping and resentment, all it took to eliminate the stupid daily wet
towel issue was an honest, non-accusatory conversation, an exploration
of the root cause, and a little joint creative problem solving.

Now that's a House That Cleans Itself in action, teamwork style.

11

Put God at the Center

STEP 8

Commit to the LORD whatever you do,
and he will establish your plans.

PROVERBS 16:3

This final step is the most important of all. I saved it for last because I knew if I put it first you might skip over it entirely in your hurry to learn about the HTCI System. I hope by now you're feeling much more oriented to the plan and are able to give this step the attention it deserves.

As you begin to implement the HTCI System in your home, it's important to place this transition in God's hands and keep Him at the center of the process. Thus, this chapter will show you how to:

1. Prayer walk your home.

2. Create a devotional area you can use from now on.

Prayer Walk Your House

Have you ever heard of "prayer walking"? That's where you take a stroll through a neighborhood or town while praying for the people in each home or business as you go by. My church strongly supports prayer walking to bathe our entire region in prayer. They even have a map of our county on which we can place pins on the streets we cover during our regular walks.

I've done plenty of prayer walking in my neighborhood, but only when I decided to get a handle on our mess and clutter did it cross my mind to prayer walk my *house*. I highly encourage you to begin the House That Cleans Itself process with an indoor prayer walk of your own. It will focus your efforts, reaffirm your priorities, and give you the opportunity to ask for God's blessings upon you and your family in very specific ways. If you've never prayer walked before, you may feel a little silly doing it at first, but do it anyway. Soon you'll be lost in the prayer itself, and your self-consciousness will fly out the window.

Just be sure that this is one prayer you give with your eyes open— lest you trip over the mess you want to clean up.

Preparing for Your Prayer Walk

Before you begin, there are a few matters to consider:

Should you do it alone or with your family? I first thought my prayer walk would be a family event, but when I mentioned it at dinner one night, I was met with blank stares and uncomfortable shrugs. My family's not usually shy when it comes to prayer, but something about going through our home and praying for each room in turn didn't appeal to them as it did to me. They thought it sounded kind of...well, odd.

For me cleaning isn't just a responsibility; it's also a mission. I needed to prayer walk my house to put God at the center of my housecleaning mission. I did the prayer walk alone. As it turned out, the time was more intense, focused, unhurried, and pleasing than it might have been had my husband and daughters shared in the experience.

Talk to your family and see what they want to do. Either way, it will be an uplifting, encouraging experience.

Choose a time that won't be interrupted. Take the phone off the hook, turn off all cell phones, and prepare to have peace and quiet for at least 30 minutes. If you have small children at home, don't do this while they are underfoot. Send them on an outing with a babysitter, relative, or friend. If that's not possible, at the very least wait until they are asleep.

Heed the words of Matthew 5:23-24: "If you are offering your gift at the altar and there remember that your brother or sister has something against you, leave your gift there in front of the altar. First go and be reconciled to them; then come and offer your gift." If you know you have issues in your life that need to be taken care of, do so now before you begin so your time with God is not hindered.

As you go, move from one end of your home to the other without missing a single room. You want to bathe every space in prayer, making sure nothing is left out.

As you take your prayer walk, ask God to show you the perfect place to set up a devotional area. You may already have a regular devotional routine that works for you, but if not, this step is vital. Somewhere in your home is a place where you can grab quiet moments on a daily basis to read God's Word and pray. When your prayer walk is over, the very next thing you'll do will be to set up this devotional area so you can take on this new habit and easily make it part of each and every day.

How to Prayer Walk a House

If you have never prayer walked before, you're probably wondering how it works. Prayer walking outside is done very discreetly, a sort of silent, running prayer to God in your mind as you walk through a neighborhood or down a city street. A prayer walk through your home, however, can be quite a different experience. Because no one is looking or listening, feel free to pray out loud, pause in different places as you feel led, raise your hands, recite Scripture, and even burst into song or dance before the Lord. Afraid you'll feel stupid? Please don't. This is between you and God, and He treasures your transparency and willingness to come to Him this way.

To get started, go to your front entryway, pause, close your eyes, and allow the quiet to envelop you. This is your time with the Lord. Don't rush it.

Begin by simply praising God. Recite a psalm of praise, or sing a refrain of "Our God Is an Awesome God," or just speak to Him with reverence and appreciation. You might read some psalms or other praise verses aloud, such as this verse from Revelation 4:11: "You are worthy, our Lord and God, to receive glory and honor and power, for you created all things, and by your will they were created and have their being."

Next, still in that same place, confess any sin that may be coming between you and your Maker. Ask God for forgiveness and allow Him to cleanse your heart. Isn't God's grace amazing? Rejoice!

Tell God how much you want to honor Him through the keeping of your home. Ask Him to bless your house and all who live in it. Give each family member to Him by name, perhaps reciting Joshua 24:15: "Choose for yourselves this day whom you will serve...But as for me and my household, we will serve the LORD." Ask God to shine His light through you and yours to all who pass through this doorway.

Now open your eyes and look around this area and pray aloud any specific concerns you have regarding its organization or cleanliness. For example, you might say, "Please help me find a way to keep everyone from dumping their sports equipment right here on the floor," or "Please help me keep from feeling resentful when my husband leaves his briefcase there on the counter." You don't need to make a laundry list of everything that's wrong with the room, but for any specific issues that pop into your head, go ahead and commit them to prayer. The God who knows the exact number of hairs on your head is happy to hear about and help with your most mundane household struggles.

Continue praying as you move to the next room. Beyond any specifics, you can ask for help in keeping the home clean, in maintaining focus and structure, in reinforcing habits, and in maintaining discipline. Ask also that the Lord help you see your trouble spots and give you ideas for how best to handle them. Ask for patience, respect, and discernment in dealing with family members as they join you in your quest for cleanliness. Ask for unconditional, limitless, grace-filled outpourings of love for all who live there.

If you reach an area and no words come to mind, sing a hymn or recite Scripture instead. As you make your way through the house, continue to bathe it in prayer. Remember to be thankful and to keep a grateful heart for all your material blessings. That we have been blessed with a house and possessions to get messy in the first place is something we often forget.

Finally, remember to ask God to keep you mindful of the main priority here, that you get past the mess so you can focus on others and live the life He intends for you to live. End your prayer walk by asking that He plant in you enthusiasm and energy for the many ways you can serve Him more once your home is under control. With that vision in mind, it's easier not to get bogged down by the work that lies ahead.

Why Prayer Walk?

Besides placing your petitions for help before the Lord, my hope is that the prayer walk will change your heart by reminding you that God's hand is on your entire home, messy or clean, under control or out of control, and that His love and purpose cover all of your shortcomings. Romans 8:31 asks, "If God is for us, who can be against us?" Truly, God is *for* you, and He wants to help you put housecleaning in its proper place—no more and no less important than it should be.

Create a Devotional Area

Once your prayer walk is complete, it's time to set up a place for daily devotions. Commit to having this special time and place with God, and before you know it a new habit will have formed.

First, ask yourself what time of day—every day—you'll be able to grab some alone time with God. It doesn't have to be extensive. If you are the mother of small children and can squeeze in only five minutes, commit to God those five minutes. He knows your heart and your situation.

Once you know the time of day you'll do your devotions, you will have a better idea of a suitable place. For example:

+ If you're going to get up early, you might not want to do it in a room that takes a while to get warm.

+ If you're going to do it while others are sleeping, you won't want to be where you might disturb them with your reading light or rustling pages.

+ If you're going to do it while people are in the house, you'll want to choose an area with a door that closes.

Ideally you should find (or set up) a comfy chair beside a good reading light. Now gather the following supplies:

+ *A Bible.* Use whatever translation and format you like best.

+ *A highlighter* if you like to mark important verses.

+ *A pen or pencil and a blank notebook or prayer journal.* Your prayer journal can be as minimal or extensive as you want it to be, but at the very least it should include a brief list of the things and people you are praying about. Update this regularly. Nothing reinforces our understanding of answered prayers better than a record of our requests and God's answers. At least once a year, maybe around New Year's Day or on your birthday, thumb through your prayer journal and marvel at God's faithfulness and ingenuity in responding to your petitions.

+ *A paper, chart, or book that shows your Bible reading schedule* if you are working through a program. Most everyone has seen typical read-the-Bible-in-a-year plans, but did you know there are also plans for reading the Bible over several years (for intensive, drawn-out study) and even for reading it in 90 days (for a fast, broad overview)? Reading through the Bible in a variety of ways can help open your mind to new truths each time.

+ *A few good devotional books.* I used to think I had to stick with one devotional for a year, but then I realized I could keep several devotionals at hand and switch back and forth between them at will. Some days I skip the devotional entirely and just focus on a Bible passage instead. Most days, though, I like the structure a devotional gives, and I choose which one I want to read based on how clear my brain feels, how deep I want to go, or where I need help. Consequently, I make sure to keep three different kinds on hand: one that offers complex and profound truths, one that's relevant to my day-to-day life, and one that's light and easy for a quick read.

+ *Any comfort items that will help to put you in a worshipful frame of mind.* Some people worship best in a setting that is austere, such as the cold stone of a monastery or in a small prayer closet. But you may be more likely to immerse yourself in the process and stay with it longer if you take a few steps to make your devotional area comfortable. God just wants you to come to Him—however you come to Him! You might include a lap blanket, a candle and matches, a small CD player with a praise music CD waiting inside, a box of tissues, a shawl, and a pillow on the floor for when you feel called to kneel. The point is to have a place that's ready and waiting for your devotional time at a moment's notice.

+ *A kitchen timer.* Yes, you need a timer if you: 1) avoid daily devotions because you know you'll get lost in them and end up spending extra time you don't have to spare, or 2) cannot truly focus on daily devotions because you are too distracted watching the clock so you'll know when to stop. Whenever possible, don't put God on a schedule, keep a tight lid on your worship time, or ignore the Holy Spirit's tugging on your heart if more prayer is needed. But if you avoid devotions because you are afraid of the time commitment, setting a timer will free you to meet with God much more often.

Whatever you choose to include in your devotion area, the goal is to set up a permanent grouping of items that do not get carried anywhere else for any other purpose.

Building the Habit

Once you have chosen the space where you plan to do your devotions and have gathered the necessary items, put everything in a tote bag or basket (or a box that locks if you want to keep your journal private). Place it within easy reach of where you'll be sitting.

Tomorrow, at the time you have decided upon, go to this place and spend at least five minutes doing your devotions. No matter how busy you are, you must have five spare minutes somewhere in your day for you to read a Bible passage and pray. The next day, try for a little longer—say, ten minutes. Slowly work your way up in time each day, if you can, but always allow yourself the freedom to spend only five minutes if that's all you have. In the past, chances are it would have taken twice as long as that just to find your Bible and gather the items you need.

How much time should you work up to? That depends on your other obligations and even your attention span, but for most people daily devotions last anywhere from five minutes to an hour, with the average being 15 to 30 minutes. During that time you can read the allotted Bible verses, read that day's page in a devotional book, write in your prayer journal, and pray.

Remember, coming to God this way is a privilege and a joy. It can take a certain amount of commitment to get rolling on this as a daily habit, but if after several weeks you find you are still doing it only out of obligation or duty, something is wrong. Speak to your pastor or a wise Christian friend to help you figure out what might be hindering your time with God. Consider also that often when prayer time does not flow and feels more like a burden than an opportunity, it may be because there is some unconfessed sin that's coming between you and God.

Finally, take time each day to read and pray, but also remember to quietly meditate and listen for God's leading. A messy house can be a noisy house, spiritually speaking, and the more you turn down that noise and focus on God, the more you can hear His voice and understand His plan for you.

Don't forget: You have an appointment in this place, at the time you have determined, every day of the week, beginning tomorrow.

Be there. Consistently.

It will have a greater impact on you, your life, and your home than you can ever imagine.

My Most Embarrassing Messy House Story
—A Corny Tale—
BY BETTY R.

I had gone to the trouble of boiling several ears of corn and slicing off the kernels to make a good-sized bowl of delicious, buttery sweet corn. Because our Bible study members wouldn't be arriving for the meal for another half hour, I put the bowl of corn in the microwave and hit the "keep warm" button. Our small group came for dinner. We enjoyed the chicken, mashed potatoes and gravy, biscuits, vegetable casserole, and dessert.

It wasn't until the next time I used the microwave—*five days later*—that I discovered the bowl of corn. All that work of cutting the kernels off those piping hot ears, and then I forgot to serve it. I was mad at myself for my absentmindedness—not to mention nauseated by the awful stench of five-day-old corn!

Part 3

Stay on Course

Let perseverance finish its work
so that you may be mature and complete,
not lacking anything.

James 1:4

12

Maintaining Your Achievement

*Our people must learn to devote themselves to doing
what is good, in order to provide for urgent needs
and not live unproductive lives.*

TITUS 3:14

There are three elements to ongoing maintenance of a House That
Cleans Itself, each of which involves the possibility of certain
types of messes happening in the future. However, you can easily
preempt these messes so that they'll never happen at all.

To do this, you must:

+ anticipate your put-away style
+ anticipate a need for container limits
+ anticipate ongoing donations

Each of the above concepts is explained below.

Anticipating Your Put-Away Style

Here's a big dose of reality for all who are housekeeping impaired:
One of the most self-deceiving and self-defeating things we do around
the house is set up systems that don't take into account our own unique
put-away styles. Your put-away style, or PAS, is the manner in which
you usually put something away when you're finished with it.

Think about it. For example, what's your PAS when it comes to extension cords? When you finish using one, do you neatly wrap the cord up before you put it back in the closet? Or do you cram it back in there in a big messy wad, thinking you'll straighten it out later? If you're housekeeping impaired, chances are it's the latter. Yet there's also a good chance that the place you've created for storing extension cords is some sort of hook or small container that will only work if the cord has been neatly wrapped up first.

My friend, it's time for a little self-awareness check. As you turn your home into a House That Cleans Itself, you must always keep in mind your PAS whenever you are designating storage spaces for anything.

A cleaning expert might say, "Oh, come on, it only takes a second to wrap up a cord before putting it away." But I say, if you were going to do that in the future, you would have already been doing it in the past. If your PAS means that nine times out of ten you cram extension cords away in a wad, then instead of denying reality—or beating yourself up about it—why not just face facts, anticipate it, and create a space for it? Then your usual action, your default PAS, will become the correct method for storage. Once again, you will have changed the house to fit the behavior, which is the goal of every House That Cleans Itself.

Years ago I kept my cords on little hooks inside the mop closet, which of course meant that most of the time they were getting thrust blindly into the closet to "fix later," falling onto the floor, and creating a jumbled mess among the mops and brooms.

Once I learned to anticipate my own personal PAS, I ditched the hook system entirely. Now there's a big bucket that sits on the floor of the same closet for just that purpose. We cram the cords into the bucket when we are done with them and pull them out from the bucket when we need them again. Our PAS determined our storage area, and it works just fine for us.

Another such item that might have a messy PAS for you is batteries. I have tried so many lovely little battery racks over the years, to no avail. When it comes to batteries, my PAS is to toss them into something, not painstakingly place them on a rack one by one. My solution was to designate a battery drawer. Inside that one drawer are packages of new batteries, loose batteries, and a battery tester. My neater friends probably have a much prettier system, but by analyzing my way of dealing with batteries and creating a space for it, I eliminated a source of mess in my home.

Where are you running into trouble with an unanticipated PAS?

+ *Socks and underwear?* Then use a drawer or container big enough that you can simply cram your socks and undies in any way you want, unfolded and unmatched. Who cares?

+ *The garden hose?* Then get a big outdoor pot and toss it in there in a wad. (Or do what I did and buy one on a big spool that you can retract by turning the handle.)

+ *Spices?* Then stop trying to use that fancy visible spice rack and toss your spice jars into a bin instead, one that hides inside a nearby kitchen cabinet.

+ *Art supplies?* Again, get a bin, one that's big enough to scoop them into, and keep it in a nearby closet or cabinet. I still wish I could get back the hours I spent when my kids were small, separating crayons from markers and putting them into the cute little art supply holder I had bought them. Like it mattered!

What else has a messy PAS in your world? Think about it and then create a system that accommodates it rather than conflicts with it. By anticipating your PAS, you can preempt—and prevent—mess all over the house.

Anticipating the Need for Container Limits

Time for another dose of reality: Sometimes those of us who are housekeeping impaired have a little trouble with excess. It's not that we *want* a five-foot high pile of old newspapers or six bushels full of used plastic grocery bags, it's just that these things sort of collect over time and we're not all that good about processing them back out of the house.

If this is an issue for you, learn to anticipate this problem by giving yourself what I call "container limits." This is when you use a designated physical space in your home to limit the total quantity of an item you're allowed to have before you must take action. For example, you might decide to own as many clothes as will fit in your closet, and if you exceed that amount you have to give some away—though whether such a limit would be realistic in your house depends on the size of your existing wardrobe, not to mention your closet.

More practical container limits are those which help you keep under control those things that tend to grow rapidly in your house. Perhaps you're not great about folding the laundry. In that case, you could use a big laundry basket, one that holds several loads of clothes. As loads come out of the dryer, you're allowed to dump them into the basket. But as soon as that basket is full, you have no choice but to sit down and fold.

My personal issue is mail-order catalogs. I love to get them, but if I'm not careful, I can be overrun in a matter of weeks. That's why I have a basket in my mail-processing area where all of my incoming catalogs are dropped. The sides of the basket are about a foot high, which means I'm allowed to collect a pretty hefty-sized pile of these things before I have to take a few minutes to weed out the duds and toss them into the recycling bucket.

Sometimes, especially as the holidays approach, the basket gets full even without any duds. At that point, I have to sit down and make some choices, tossing good catalogs I'm not planning to order from this time around, eliminating duplicates, and winnowing things back down to the limits of my container.

No one is standing over me, forcing me to follow my own rule, but because I know the messy consequences of this tendency toward excess, I allow the container to dictate that point in time when I must take action.

If you can identify the things in your home that tend to build up to unreasonable amounts, consider giving yourself container limits—and then sticking to them from here on out. It's a fairly painless way to avoid mess and help preserve your House That Cleans Itself.

Anticipating Donations

In chapter 8, "Aim for Simplicity," we talked about a new mind-set for eliminating clutter throughout your home. Hand in hand with that concept goes this one: Because de-cluttering is an ongoing process and not just a one-time event, you need a system for taking those items out of your house on a regular basis.

Say you have a pair of slacks you no longer want and have decided to give away. If you're housekeeping impaired, you would probably set those slacks aside, intending to donate them, but before you would have a chance to do anything with them, they would just end up getting lost in the clutter again. In a House That Cleans Itself, however, there's a simple solution to this problem. You can anticipate this need by providing an easy way to process donations straight out the door. Do this by setting up one or two permanent "charity buckets" in your home—essentially clean, lidded bins, baskets, or trash cans lined with plastic bags—and any time you run across something you no longer want or need, simply place it inside this container. Items may accumulate quickly or slowly, but the key to making the system work is the follow-through: When the bucket is full, simply pull out the plastic bag filled with your donations, tie it off, and get it to its final destination.

Most homes only need one or two charity buckets. We have two: one for upstairs, which we keep on the floor of the linen closet, and one for downstairs, which we keep just inside the interior door to the garage. Our upstairs bucket is the size of a tall kitchen trash can, but our downstairs one is much bigger, the size of an outdoor garbage can. That way we can purge items large and small with ease.

Set up one or two handy charity buckets in your home, and because you've already done your homework about who accepts what sorts of items, you already know what to take where and when.

13

Sample Stations

When God gives someone wealth and possessions,
and the ability to enjoy them,
to accept their lot and be happy in their toil—
this is a gift of God.

ECCLESIASTES 5:19

In chapter 7, "Think like a Hotel," we talked about eliminating rabbit trails by setting up stations throughout your home. Following are some additional examples of common stations and the items you may want to include in them.

Making a Pot of Coffee

If you're in the habit of making coffee, it stands to reason that everything you need should be in the cabinet nearest your coffeemaker. This includes mugs, cups, saucers, sugar, sweetener, nondairy creamer, coffee, filters, measuring scoop, and anything else that's part of your coffee routine. For stirring, keep a few extra teaspoons in the same cabinet so you don't have to go to the silverware drawer, or buy a box of plastic stirrers at a discount or office supply store. If you like to take your coffee to go, include insulated mugs or cups with lids.

Doing Homework

Most kids gravitate to the place where they like doing homework best. My girls used to rotate between the kitchen table, the computer desk, and the big comfy chair in the family room, depending on what sort of homework they were doing.

For years I dreamed of giving them neat matching desks in their bedrooms, well lit and filled with the latest office and art supplies. But the more I read about successful homework routines and strategies, the more I was convinced that most kids do best when they can work in a quiet and peaceful environment with a parent nearby. As it turns out, we were on the right track all those years when they did their homework in the kitchen while I cooked dinner. According to many experts, that's one of the best setups going.

Wherever your kids do their homework, establish a homework station that's easily accessible to that place. Depending on the ages of your kids, a homework station may include all sorts of school supplies, such as lined paper, white paper, pens, pencils, colored pencils, markers, crayons, glue sticks, tape, correction tape, a three-hole punch, hole reinforcers, extra folders and spiral notebooks, notecards, a calculator, construction paper, stapler, staples, highlighters, Post-it Notes, a dictionary, thesaurus, study Bible, and foreign language dictionary. (Larger items, such as poster boards and foamcore boards, may need to be stored elsewhere, perhaps behind a bookshelf so they won't get bent.) Work with your children to find out what they need, but don't oversupply them. If the homework station is too cluttered, you'll end up with another mess.

Depending on how much stuff is required, you may be able to keep everything in a tote bag or it may take several shelves in a cabinet or bookcase. As long as you stock everything your kids need but nothing they don't, you'll be in good shape. If you think they can handle it, put them in charge of keeping an inventory and ask them to let you know whenever something needs to be replaced.

Charging Electronics

You need to locate your charging station near an out-of-the-way outlet so you won't have to look at it or bump into it all the time. However, it also must be near enough to the center of action that family members will walk over and plug in their phones, cameras, and iPods. The closer this place is to the main door your family usually goes in and out of, the better.

Your charging station can be anything from a fancy store-bought model with wood trim and a recessed bottom to a simple power strip. The key is to use whatever system looks nice and neat and helps you avoid cord clutter, as shown:

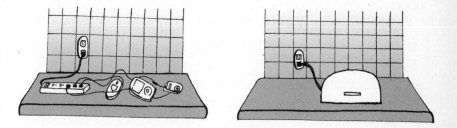

One final tip: If you do much traveling, save yourself some trouble and purchase duplicate phone chargers for your trips. That way, you don't have to mess up your charging station by digging those chargers out every time you go away.

Getting Ready for Church

This may seem like an unusual item to include, but think about that mad, last-minute rush when you can't find your Sunday school book or your son's Bible or your tithing envelopes. I truly believe that one of Satan's favorite tools to use against Christian families is to make chaos out of our mornings when we are trying to get ready for church. Those dumb little arguments that spring up as we run around preparing to leave can result in irritated parents, sullen kids, and hearts that are in no way ready for worshipping or learning.

For the next month, as your family gets ready for church, pay attention to the items that are causing problems, and then compile those into a churchgoing station. You'll probably end up with a mix of emergency items that can be used in a pinch, such as an extra hairbrush, a new pack of pantyhose or knee-highs, a pair of men's black socks, and a spare Bible. Also include your Sunday school books, tithing envelopes, blank checks, and a pen. If your church has a lending library, this would also be a good place to keep the items you've checked out that are ready for return.

Getting Ready for a Workout

There's a good reason you need to set up this station: If your workout involves little or no necessary prep time, you'll be more likely to follow through. How many times have you skipped a workout because it was too much trouble to pull things together?

If you work out solely at a gym or the Y, your gym bag is your workout station. Make sure it includes all personal equipment you need, such as goggles, earplugs, swim cap, towel, water bottle, and lock for the locker. Be sure to include duplicates of the items you need for showering and doing your hair and makeup so you never have to grab those things from your shower and dressing area at home. I can't tell you how many years I spent with one bottle of deodorant shuttled back and forth between gym bag and bathroom until I finally had one of those forehead-slapping "Duh!" moments. It's amazing how having two bottles of deodorant made my life so much simpler. Ditto for shampoo, conditioner, and other necessary toiletries.

To keep your workout station current, make a habit of replacing certain items as soon as you get home from the gym, such as towel, water bottle, clean socks and underwear, rather than waiting until it's time to go again. That way your gym bag is ready to grab at a moment's notice.

If you do your workouts at home, your workout station may involve equipment such as a treadmill, free weights, or simply the television, exercise DVDs, and open floor space. If you do your exercising outside, you might use a good pair of sneakers, a portable radio, a tennis racket, a can of balls, a basketball, a volleyball, a hockey stick, and a pair of skates.

Whatever your home equipment needs are, be sure to think through your entire workout. Remember to include every item you might want, such as Band-Aids for blisters, a knee or ankle brace if helpful, an air pump for your basketball or bicycle tires, a water bottle, a visor, sports sunglasses, and sunscreen. Depending on how much room this station takes up, you may end up using anything from a small tote bag to an entire closet.

To keep outdoor sporting equipment from overtaking your home, establish two distinct areas: your workout station, which holds your current sporting equipment and supplies, and your sporting goods storage, which holds the equipment you use at other times during the year. Your sporting goods storage needs to be easily accessible, such as in a garage or shed, but out of the way of general traffic. This is especially important if you are heavily involved in winter sports and summer sports. Skis, sleds, snowboards, and other equipment can take up an enormous amount of room and should be stored far out of the way in the off-season. My husband keeps our skis and sleds above the garage, stacked along the rafters, until the first snowflakes fall.

Even if you're good about putting away the off-season equipment, you still may have trouble accommodating all of the current stuff. One resourceful mother I know solved her problem of having three sons in three different sports in a very clever way. Because each kid needed his own workout station, she bought three full-sized metal lockers. She put the lockers in a row in the garage, right beside the door, and told the boys their available equipment could not exceed the interior space of the lockers. That forced them to weed out bulky, off-season items, such as hockey sticks and football pads, and move them to the sporting goods storage area when they weren't in use. The locker system worked so well that eventually she added a fourth locker. The bottom portion was used to store the air pump and other communal items they played with in their yard year-round, such as a basketball, a softball, and a bat. The top portion was reserved for her own workout station, which consisted primarily of a helmet, pads, and a pair of roller blades. Once she no longer had to dig around the garage and the shed to pull her things together, she used them far more often.

Getting Ready to Travel

As a family we travel so much that we have dedicated an entire closet as our travel station. It holds all of our suitcases and sleeping bags. Inside is also a plastic shelving unit with clear, removable bins that contain duplicate chargers for our phones and cameras, travel-sized toiletries (usually extras brought home from hotels), tote bags, luggage tags and straps, a variety of cloth and plastic zippered bags (most acquired over the years with free gifts from the Clinique counter), disposable cameras, two different-sized boxes of baggies, nifty travel tools (such as a small portable fan), an adapter kit, a travel alarm clock, and more.

Our maps, atlases, and travel books are kept in a different place, as are our passports, so not every item we need for travel is in that one closet, but we have been able to come pretty close. Certainly, getting ready for a trip is much easier than it used to be.

If you hardly ever travel, you may not need a travel station. On the other hand, if you or a family member travel constantly, take your travel station to the next level and keep a packed bag in your closet at all times. I know one woman who is a professional speaker and author and has engagements and appearances 30 to 40 weekends per year. Her bag is literally never unpacked. As soon as she returns from one trip, she replaces any used-up items in her bag, packs it with the clothes she'll need for her next trip, and then puts it into the closet. At the end of the week, when it's time for her to leave again, she can grab her bag, add any last-minute items, and go. The reason this works for her is because she buys clothes that are specifically made not to wrinkle. I didn't really believe there were such things until she convinced me to buy one wrinkle-free outfit for myself. Now I'll never travel with anything else. Surf the web for "wrinkle-free clothing," and you'll find a number of options from a variety of suppliers.

Making Small Household Repairs

Chances are your home has two types of tools: the everyday stuff, such as hammers and screwdrivers, and the more involved things, such as band saws and belt sanders. Most folks, even messy folks, are fairly organized about these bigger tools and are able to keep track of them because the tools are unlikely to get carried to other places around the house. (My kids may unthinkingly run off with my tape measure, but I doubt they'll ever misplace the chain saw.)

It's not difficult to set up a heavy-duty tool station in a garage or shed and then duplicate some of the minor tools for an indoor repair station. What that repair station includes depends entirely on how handy you are and how likely you are to want at your fingertips mid-level tools, such as drills and electric screwdrivers.

At our house my husband handles everything more complicated than hammering in a nail. He likes to keep his tools together in one place, so all I have in our repair station are duplicate items of the most common things, including a hammer; an assortment of screwdrivers (big and small, Phillips and regular); pliers; a wrench; an assortment of nails, screws, hooks, and picture hangers; a carpenter's measure; a small level; and a roll of duct tape. Your repair station may have more items in it than mine, but the key is to fill it only with things you will use regularly and not anything you only need two or three times a year.

What rabbit trails are wasting time and causing clutter for you? Use these examples of common stations to streamline all sorts of routine processes in your home.

My Most Embarrassing Messy House Story
—Time for a Change—
BY EVELYN R.

Grandma dropped by for a scheduled visit. I'd cleaned and delegated jobs to the children, one of whom had forgotten to put away the vacuum cleaner. (This wasn't an issue. At least it proved we vacuumed on occasion.) But the brand caught Grandma's eye, and she walked toward it and grasped the handle.

"Is this one of those light little eight-pound vacuums?" she asked.

I nodded and smiled just as Grandma tried to lift it—and couldn't.

"Good grief! That's a lot more than eight pounds!"

I grabbed the handle. A churning in my stomach reminded me that I'd given all vacuuming responsibility to my 12-year-old, and I hadn't checked the bag in ages. Gulping at the gritty gray trail of dust that followed any movement of the handle, I wrestled it to the front porch. It weighed at least 30 pounds! I unzipped the bag and engulfed my grandma, mom, and me in a cloud of dirt.

Grandma still laughs ten years later. The vacuum still works...if I remember to change the bag.

14

Releasing Your Grip

*Good will come to those who are generous and lend
freely, who conduct their affairs with justice.*

PSALM 112:5

In chapter 8, "Aim for Simplicity," I described how to purge clutter from your home. Even if you're not quite ready for a house-wide de-cluttering, you might find specific types of focused purges—or, to use more upbeat terminology, "releases"—helpful, including a:

+ lifestyle release
+ technology release
+ habit release
+ collection release
+ frenzy release
+ the great eBay self-deception release
+ duplication release
+ delegated release

Each of these concepts is explained below.

Lifestyle Release

Do this kind of de-cluttering when something about your lifestyle has changed—for example, when your baby years are over and you no longer need those high chairs and cribs, or when you know for certain your youngest child won't be playing with certain categories of toys any more. (Bye-bye, Legos and Barbies!) One of my biggest lifestyle releases came when we no longer hosted Thanksgiving. For years we welcomed up to 25 members of my husband's family into our home annually, which meant I had built up a collection of all sorts of platters, warmers, cookers, table linens, and more. Eventually, we passed that mantle over to my husband's brother and his wife, along with many of the items we knew they would need. But it didn't dawn on me for another seven or eight years after that, that the rest of my "Thanksgiving hostess collection" was still cluttering up my storage area—and that it was all stuff I would more than likely never use again. In one fell swoop, I filled several big boxes with these items I no longer needed, thanks to a change in my lifestyle, and donated them to a local shop kitchen.

Technology Release

Thanks to advances in technology, in many ways we live differently now than we did even just a few years ago. From e-readers to digital downloads, many electronic devices are rendering some of our possessions obsolete—and this is a trend that will continue.

It amazes me, for example, how much my old packing list has shrunk in the past few years. Thanks to my smartphone, when I travel these days, I no longer need to bring along books, CD player, CDs, DVDs, flashlight, maps, camera, guidebooks, address book, notepad, digital voice recorder, magnifying glass, or Bible. When I first realized this, it astounded me how technology had made each of these items unnecessary. That realization led me to do a technology release throughout my home.

Perhaps it's time you did one too. Consider de-cluttering books, videos, tapes, albums, CDs, appliances, telephone books, and more. As times change and we all go more digital, keep your eyes open for ways you can clear out the clutter for good.

Habit Release

This is a simple one. Has a habit of yours changed, but you haven't yet adapted the house for that change? Sometimes you can do a quick release of the items connected with the old, outgrown habit.

For example, perhaps you switched from using the front door each day to going in and out through the garage instead, yet you still have umbrellas, jackets, and tote bags cluttering the area around the front door.

Or maybe you used to eat ice cream every night, a habit that you eventually managed to ditch. Perhaps it's time to ditch those cute ice cream bowls, scoops, and jars of sauces as well.

Collection Release

Collectors are usually tough nuts to crack, but this release idea is worth a mention. If you have a collection of some kind that you *might* be willing to part with but can't quite let go, consider trying this clever idea. Dust and clean that collection till it sparkles, photograph each item, and then use an online photo service to create a photo book featuring the items in the collection. That way, you can go ahead and get rid of the collection but you'll always have the pictures to remind you of it.

And chances are a photo book—even a deluxe hardback size—will take up far less space than the original collection ever did.

Frenzy Release

What gets you in the mood to purge clutter? For me, it's a visit with a beloved relative who happens to be a hoarder. I adore the time we spend together, but whenever I come back from staying with her, I'm ready to get rid of half of everything I own.

I've learned through experience to seize the mood by seizing the day. After several hours of frenzied de-cluttering, my house looks better and I feel much more at peace.

When you're in the mood to clear things out, for whatever reason, take advantage of it. Grab boxes and bags, put on some fast-paced music, and get busy. Even half an hour of dedicated de-cluttering can go a long way toward creating a House That Cleans Itself.

The Great eBay Self-Deception Release

Do you allow yourself to stockpile certain items with the excuse that you plan to sell them on eBay someday? That's fine if you're already an active eBay seller and you're just dealing with a temporary inventory overload.

But if you've never even registered as a user, chances are your dreams of eBay riches are an excuse, not a real intention. If you've been skating by on this one, it's time to fish or cut bait. Give yourself a deadline to list the item, put that deadline on the calendar, and stick to it.

If the date arrives and you haven't yet posted the item for sale, then you have no choice but to get rid of it in more conventional ways instead. While eBay can be a great tool for some people, more often than not it's simply an excuse to hang on to something for the housekeeping impaired. Be honest enough with yourself not to fall into this trap.

Duplication Release

What do you have more than one of in your home? Possibilities include:

+ yardsticks
+ brooms
+ mops
+ fly swatters
+ cooking implements
+ small appliances
+ household tools
+ beauty implements

Keep your eyes open for unnecessary duplications and make a point to ditch the doubles.

Delegated Release

Even your smallest family members may have possessions they no longer want or need. Challenge your children to find ten things in their room or playroom to give away. You may be surprised to see how quickly and easily they are able to do just that.

Then let them be a part of blessing someone else with those items. If they are old enough to sort through their possessions, they are certainly old enough to experience the joy of helping others.

15

Your Home Base Zone

I have no peace, no quietness;
I have no rest, but only turmoil.

Job 3:26

Years ago when my daughters were small and money was tight, we lived for a while in an old house that had almost no closets, an unusable basement, and very little in the way of storage. The place was usually a mess. I couldn't get a handle on my time, my organization, my clutter, or my cleaning. Consequently, most days I felt frustrated and discouraged.

At that time a wise friend sensed my desperation and offered some advice that I have used to this day: *When you can't get a handle on anything else in your house, figure out that one place that most affects you emotionally, clean it up, and keep it clean no matter what.* She said that everyone has some place in their home that is important to them in a unique way, and when it's clean they feel an inordinate amount of satisfaction, and when it's dirty they feel an inordinate amount of irritation and stress.

Do you know what that place might be for you?

For Martha Cilley, the Internet's household-wisdom-dispensing "FlyLady," that area is her kitchen sink (check out www.flylady.net). Cilley's entire housekeeping makeover, in fact, begins with her directive to get into your kitchen, clean your sink, and keep it sparkling. While I agree with her idea in theory, I suggest that one woman's sink may be another woman's toilet. Only *you* know what that one thing is in your home that most brings you peace if it's kept spotless. It may be your kitchen sink, but it may be something entirely different.

For me, I finally decided that special place was the upstairs bathroom. For some reason I'll never be able to explain, when that room was strewn with wet towels and dirty clothes and in need of a good scrubbing and mopping, I felt overwhelmed beyond comprehension. Conversely, on those rare occasions in the past when I had attacked that room with vigor and made it sparkle, I felt strangely calm and proud. Sometimes when it was clean, I would even stand in the doorway just to look at it and feel happy.

My friend was right. Following her advice, I made that little bathroom my cleaning priority. Sure enough, even when the whole house was a cluttered mess from one end to the other, as long as that bathroom was neat and clean, I knew all was not lost.

When I developed and refined the HTCI System, I dubbed this special sanity-saving area the "home base zone" (HBZ). You may not realize it, but you have an HBZ in your home too. To figure out where yours is, think about what bothers you the most when it's a mess and makes you the happiest when it's clean.

What's your HBZ? Here are some of the responses I have received from this question:

+ "My bed. As long as the bed is made, I'm happy."
+ "My kitchen."
+ "The counter by the back door."
+ "The inside of my car."
+ "My shed."
+ "The part of the basement we use as a pantry."
+ "The front porch."
+ "The kitchen floor. I can't stand to have a dirty or sticky kitchen floor."

+ "My home office."

+ "The toilets in all the bathrooms."

+ "The area that surrounds my easy chair in the den."

+ "The part of the laundry room where everybody dumps stuff when they come in the back door."

As you can see, there is no right answer, except the answer that's right for you. If you can't think of where your home base zone might be, ask your family to venture some guesses. Chances are, someone else might be able to tell you what you haven't been able to figure out yourself.

Once you know what and where your HBZ is, the next step is to completely strip it of all unnecessary items and clutter, and then scrub it until it shines. No, I'm not kidding. In a book that's supposed to tell you how to get your house to clean itself, I am suggesting that you get down on your hands and knees and do some deep cleaning the old-fashioned way. Depending on what and where your zone is, that can mean vacuuming, wiping, mopping, hosing off, and/or hand scrubbing. Whatever it takes, clean your zone as thoroughly as possible. When you are finished, purge any clutter and arrange the remaining items in a neat and orderly fashion.

Now that you have defined your HBZ, rid it of everything except what absolutely has to be there, and cleaned it until it shines, allow that sense of peace and accomplishment to spur you on to tackle other areas of your home as well.

My Most Embarrassing Messy House Story
—The Tale of the Missing Vandals—
BY PETER M.

One night my roommate and I went to the movies. While we were gone, some friends came over to our apartment to hang out.

When they realized we weren't at home, they thought it would be funny to play a joke on us. They put all of our furniture on the front porch in a big, upside-down pile, and left a "ha-ha" note on the door. Unfortunately, that note blew away before we got back.

When we came home we didn't realize a joke was played. We thought we had been vandalized. Scared to go inside, we called the police. They came and entered the apartment, searching throughout for signs of the intruders. When they came back out, they announced that the vandals were gone now, but obviously they had been inside the apartment and torn it apart.

"You'll have to come in and make a full report," they told us. "There are clothes all over, papers, all kinds of stuff. They totally destroyed the place."

When we went in, we saw that aside from the furniture being moved outside, nothing else had been touched. The disastrous mess the cops talked about was the mess we lived in every day!

16

The Laundry Quandary

*I delight greatly in the LORD; my soul rejoices in my
God. For he has clothed me with garments of salvation
and arrayed me in a robe of his righteousness,
as a bridegroom adorns his head like a priest,
and as a bride adorns herself with her jewels.*

Why is laundry such an ongoing challenge for so many? I have a few ideas. It's because:

+ it's a never-ending battle

+ most of us have too many clothes

+ if ignored it can snowball

+ if wet it can stink or mold or worse

+ someone once decided that the best place for washers and dryers was in the basement, despite the fact that most people get dressed and undressed two floors away

+ one mistake (red shirt accidentally tossed in with the whites, perhaps) can ruin an entire load

+ so many of our clothes require special treatment.

+ there are too many rules about doing it "right" that we think we ought to follow

I don't have solutions for all of the above, but I do think that half of all laundry issues would be solved if everyone would just move their washers and dryers next to their bedrooms.

I mean, really, why do we lug the dirty clothes all the way down just to wash, fold, and lug them back up? I'll tell you why: I think it's because traditionally men designed houses and women did the laundry. Now that a more equal representation is in the workforce—not to mention more men doing their share at home—you would think this would change with every new house that's built. But it isn't. Why? I'm not sure, but maybe because we are all creatures of habit, and if it was good enough for Mom this way, it should be okay for us too. I say, let's start a revolution. Washers and dryers should be as close to the place where the people in your house dress and undress as possible. In a House That Cleans Itself, this is one modification you should take under serious consideration.

Until then, here are some less drastic suggestions to try.

Sorting Dirty Laundry

How do you sort your dirty laundry? If you follow conventional wisdom, you use the standard light–medium–dark divisions the experts recommend. If you'd like to know a better way, however, consider perfecting the art of sorting in your home by doing it the House That Cleans Itself way.

Here's how it works. Take a look at your laundry with fresh eyes and think about it in terms of how you usually process it. What thoughts run through your mind when you look through the pile of what needs washing?

- ✦ *I'll need to get this clean as soon as possible.*
- ✦ *These things might have stuff in the pockets. Don't forget to check.*
- ✦ *This stuff is damp, I need to wash it before it starts to stink.*
- ✦ *I'll have to remember to hang up these shirts as soon as they're dry.*

+ *I'll need to hand wash these.*

+ *I won't be wearing this again anytime soon.*

And so on. If this is how your mind works, then why not sort your laundry this way? Instead of three bins for lights, mediums, and darks, get four or six or eight or whatever you need, and label each one with the type of dirty laundry it should hold:

+ Need ASAP

+ Check Pockets First

+ Damp

+ Hang Up Right Away

+ Special Care Needed

+ No Hurry on These

This way, when you start a load of laundry, you know exactly how it ought to be processed. Let's say it's Sunday evening and you have a busy week ahead. Better to throw in the *Damp* stuff or the *Need ASAP* stuff now, because you might not get around to doing laundry again until Friday.

I have six laundry divisions in my home: *Lights, Darks, Fleece, Special Care Needed* (mostly my dressier clothes), *Hang Up Right Away* (mostly my husband's dress shirts), and *Don't Put in Dryer* (mostly my husband's T-shirts). Those last three distinctions are to prevent problems:

+ I don't want my husband washing my *Special Care Needed* clothes because, as wonderful as he is, he's not good at reading instruction tags.

+ I don't want to wash any permanent press unless I know I'll be around to hang the clothes up when they are done.

+ I'll only wash the things that get drip-dried if there's room on the dryer rack and I don't mind having stuff hang in the laundry area for a day or two. (In other words, when I know company isn't coming over any time soon.)

By sorting in a way that works with how I do loads of laundry, I've made the whole process less problematic and more efficient.

Oh, Those Clean Dirty Clothes

Judging by my reader mail, the biggest laundry issue most of us face is how to deal with the ongoing dilemma of what I call the "clean dirty clothes." These are clothing items that have been worn once but are still clean enough to wear again.

Ask an expert this question, and he or she will likely look at you, perplexed, and say that you hang them up and return them to the closet. Well, that solution may work for them but it doesn't work for me and probably not for you either. We poor housekeeping-impaired folks simply cannot, will not, hang up worn-but-still-clean clothes in our closet among the clean-but-not-yet-worn stuff. I don't know why.

Perhaps this resistance has to do with either our perfectionism or our need to categorize. Whatever the cause, just the thought of it gives me the shivers. Not only do I not want my clean and dirty clothes to comingle, there's also something about the act of hanging or folding a worn item that just feels distasteful. (I suspect that feeling stems from my general forgetfulness; if the item looks newly clean, I'm likely to forget I already wore it once.)

Unfortunately, without a viable alternative for how to handle these items, they ultimately end up you know where: on the floor, where all good clean dirty clothes go to die on their way back to the dirty clothes hamper.

So what are we to do if our only choices are the floor or the closet? I suggest you create another choice—an intermediate station, if you will—for all of those clean dirty clothes. This can be a deep drawer, a row of hooks or pegs in an out-of-sight place, or even a free-standing coatrack tucked in a corner of your room.

I know that wall pegs and coatracks covered in worn clothing aren't the most beautiful sights in the world, but they are still better than draping things on chairs or plopping them on the floor. Best of all, this approach will allow you to keep those clothes relatively wrinkle-free until you have the chance to wear them again.

Additional Tips

Here are some more handy suggestions as you deal with the laundry quandaries in your house:

+ If you find it difficult to force yourself to fold clothes as they come out of the dryer, consider putting a small TV or CD player in the laundry room. When the issue is a simple boredom, five minutes of folding goes a lot faster when done to a favorite show or song.

+ Don't be a perfectionist when it comes to folding. If this tends to be a problem for you, then do a "folding presort" where you divide the clean laundry into several piles, such as "must be perfect" (dress clothes, slacks), "can be okay" (such as jeans and T-shirts), and "just get it done" (such as baby clothes and kids' play clothes). Start with the sloppiest pile first, and by the time you get to that "must be perfect" pile, chances are you'll be so tired of folding that you'll move through it more quickly than ever before.

+ Buy one kind of sock per color, not ten or twenty different styles. That way, they never need to be sorted. They can just get dumped into the drawer and pulled at random, and they'll always match.

+ Unless it's important to you for some reason, stop folding underwear. The wrinkles will smooth out as soon as you pull it on anyway.

+ Give each member of the family his or her own color for sheets and towels and make them responsible for folding and storing them. This is especially helpful with teens who tend to use a towel once and then toss.

+ When you wash and dry bed linens, slide the folded

sheets and one pillowcase into the other matching pillowcase. Store your sheet sets this way for easy grab and go.

+ Keep in mind that folding always looks much neater when it's done against a flat surface rather than in the air. I never could figure out why my housekeeper's folding was so much better than mine until I realized she was smoothing each item out on a tabletop as she folded. I, on the other hand, was standing in the middle of the room, folding things in front of me without benefit of a surface. There is a marked difference in results.

My Most Embarrassing Messy House Story
—A Nasty Surprise—
BY RITA P.

One time I brought my car to have it hand-detailed because it was so filthy and was starting to have an odor. When I went to pick it up, the man told me it wasn't ready yet. He brought me outside and showed me the problem.

Apparently some time back my toddler had dropped a bottle of milk, and it had rolled under the front passenger seat. In the time since, not only had the milk soured, but the bottle had leaked, drawing flies. I about died when I saw that the detailers had to remove the entire seat to clean under it because the whole floor was covered in maggots.

17

The Messy Entryway

*The LORD will watch over your coming and going
both now and forevermore.*

PSALM 121:8

One the biggest household issues faced by the housekeeping impaired is the challenge of the messy entryway. At its core, I think this is because we don't give enough respect to the enormity and variety of tasks this area of our home must encompass.

The place where your family members go in and out each day, however, is one of vital importance. It is a place that requires efficient organization, a good flow, cleanliness, and convenience and should contain the possessions you take in and out with you, other needed supplies, reminders, equipment, and more. No wonder so many of us find this area challenging.

This chapter offers tips on dealing with the messy entryway the House That Cleans Itself way.

Create a Launching Pad

In an ideal "launching pad," there should be a bookcase, cabinet, or shelving unit somewhere near the door, one that holds as many baskets or bins as there are family members. (This needn't be unattractive. Many stylish, high-end stores sell units for just this purpose.) Each person uses his or her bin to place items he will need to take with him when he goes out again. For Mom, that might be her purse, sunglasses, and library books; for Dad, outbound mail or dry cleaning; for kids, lunchboxes, school papers, and class projects.

If these bins are located near the door, using them is not a difficult habit to cultivate at all. Just make sure the shortest members of your family can reach the bins that have been assigned to them. If your entryway is in a less visible area (for example, your family goes in and out of the house primarily through a mudroom), you may prefer to use open cubbies or clear bins rather than the more decorative ones you would use near a front door. That way everyone can see their items and will be less likely to forget them. The whole "out of sight, out of mind" issue has always been one of my biggest problems with regard to being launched. Opaque bins or baskets simply didn't work for me because I would forget to look inside and take out the items I needed for the day. Clear baskets were the solution.

Because of her need to be able to see the items she is supposed to take with her, Carly has set up her launching pad in a jelly cabinet

 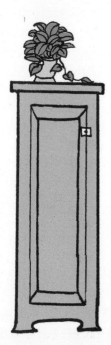

that sits beside her front door. Everyone has been given his or her own shelf inside the cabinet, and Carly applied adhesive cork to the inside of the cabinet door so that extra reminders could be pinned there like on a bulletin board. Most of the time Carly leaves the door open so everyone can see their stuff and have their memories jogged. If company comes knockin', all they do is shut the door to that cabinet and their entryway instantly looks neat.

Streamline Your Entryway

More tips on streamlining your entryway include:

+ If there's no room inside to store sporting equipment, consider placing an all-weather storage bench just *outside* the door. That may be close enough to the launching area that your little leaguers will remember to use it without much extra effort at all.

+ Store gloves, scarves, and other winter wear in a clear plastic or vinyl shoe organizer, the kind with pockets that hangs on the back of a door. (Mine has 24 pockets, and I bought it at a discount store for $15.) Place a pair of gloves (and its matching scarf, if applicable) in each pocket. Clamp clothespins on several of the pockets for use with gloves that are damp. (Rather than shoving them into the plastic pocket, clamp them so they hang outside the pocket to dry first.) This creates a winter weather station that's easy to use and tends to stay much neater than any other method I've seen.

+ Do you have hooks on which to hang keys, but no one is using them? If so, you may be surprised at the reason. Believe it or not, in this world there are hook people and there are nonhook people. If the key hooks are not getting used, chances are it's because the nonhook people in the house subconsciously think it's too much trouble. (Nonhook people have to *focus* and *think* in order to use a hook, which distracts and confuses them for a moment, causing them to lose momentum. Over time they stop seeing hooks so they won't have to pause and think about using them.)

Replacing the hooks with a small basket might solve the problem. If there's no tabletop on which to place the basket, try using the kind of basket that hangs from the wall. Just make sure it's only big enough to hold keys and nothing else, or people might begin to use it for other things as well. You may be surprised at how a simple change—like switching from a hook to a basket—can eliminate the entire keys-piled-on-the-counter problem.

✦ To prevent as much dirt as possible from being tracked into your home, always have two welcome mats, one outside with a rough texture to take off the heavy-duty grime, and one inside, perhaps a washable floor rug, for a secondary measure. Make sure each of these rugs is as big as your space can accommodate without detracting from the decor. The more times a shoe strikes a mat while walking, the more dirt will come off that shoe before it can be tracked into the rest of the house.

✦ In this era of deep-tread sneakers, welcome mats are more overworked than ever before. If the dirt coming into your home continues to be a problem, consider taking these extra steps:

Add a boot scraper near the door. (My neighbor has a cute one that looks like a porcupine.)

Put an open shoe rack or basket just inside the door, and train friends and family to remove their shoes as soon as they come inside. To make them more likely to use it, place a bench or chair nearby so they have somewhere to sit as they take off their shoes. You might also consider providing slippers, flip-flops, and other indoor-only shoes for the ones who don't want to go barefoot.

BEFORE

AFTER

My Most Embarrassing Messy House Story
—Cereal Killer—

BY MARTI T.

The kitchen counter was cluttered with dirty dishes, the evening newspaper, and a pile of mail as I hurriedly prepared the evening meal. We were expecting company so, as was generally the case with me, I went into frantic mode. Grabbing an empty Wheaties box, I swept a mound of potato peelings, carrot shavings, and the skin from a couple of large onions into the carton and set the box aside, thinking to toss it into the trash later. However, in my haste to straighten up the clutter, I forgot about the garbage in the box and quickly put the Wheaties box back where it belonged—on a shelf in the cupboard.

A full week later I was in the living room thumbing through a magazine when my husband went for a nightly snack—a bowl of cereal. Unfortunately, he was in the mood for Wheaties, so he poured himself a big bowl of...a putrid, rotting mess.

He never lets me hear the end of it.

Mind over Matter

If anyone is in Christ, the new creation has come:
The old has gone, the new is here!

2 CORINTHIANS 5:17

I t's time to address two important elements of your HTCI journey:

1. Preventing discouragement.

2. Exploring the possibility of contributing factors.

Each of the above will be explained in this chapter in turn.

Preventing Discouragement

Part of chapter 4, "Become a Detective," involved using a camera to take photos of your mess. In that chapter I said there were three reasons to do so. The first reason, *to help with the evidence-gathering process*, was explained in that section. Let's talk about the other two reasons now.

The second reason the HTCI System involves taking photos is *to give you a tangible record of your progress*. Like having before-and-after pictures when you've been on a diet, sometimes when you're starting to feel discouraged about how much more there still is to do when converting your home to a House That Cleans Itself, the very best boost available is to see just how far you've come. Take a look at those photos, and you may just be surprised at what you have already managed to accomplish.

The day I began my own HTCI conversion in earnest, my home was in an especially bad state from one end to the other, but I bravely took out my camera and started snapping pictures. The only reason I did so was to help with that first step of gathering evidence. It wasn't until much later that I realized what an encouragement they could be to me as well. Even now, as embarrassing as those pictures still are, I treasure them because they are proof positive that the HTCI System works. We may still have the occasional mess, but only when I look back at how things used to be around here do I understand how drastically things have changed. Even in occasional periods of prolonged neglect (due to book deadlines or extended travel or simply too much family life converging at once), I'm amazed to see that when I return my attention to the house, it may need a good vacuuming or mopping, but the *disaster* isn't there anymore. The floors are clear; the kitchen is functional; the bedrooms need no pathways carved through them. At those times, I feel like a successful levee builder after a storm. The levee held! The system works!

The third reason the HTCI System involves taking photos is *to use as a tool to help you limit the scope of your problem and keep it from overwhelming you.* When you think of your entire house and the mess it contains and the de-cluttering process you may be facing, the job ahead can feel enormous. But if you can frame the process in terms of each separate area contained within a photo, the task is not so daunting. Even if you don't have the time or energy to weed out an entire house, you can handle everything that is shown in a single picture, right?

This tendency to get overwhelmed was Beatrice's biggest problem with regard to clutter. She lived alone in a house that held 2500 square feet of stuff, a lifetime of accumulation she wanted to go through and clear out. But just thinking about processing room after room of possessions was so exhausting she was too discouraged to even give it a try.

Maybe some folks can't see the forest for the trees, but poor Beatrice couldn't see the trees for the forest. Taking photos throughout the house helped her focus on the smaller zones that needed attention. As long as she tackled her stuff one photo's worth at a time, she was able to keep going without wanting to give up. Eventually she made her way through her entire house. She kept more items than I would have (Beatrice has yet to deal with her psychological need to hoard), but she still managed to send five minivan loads of boxes and furniture to a local thrift store.

If the job ahead of you seems far too large to handle, I suggest you follow her example. Store your pictures in an album in your smartphone or stick the prints in a notebook or photo book in the order you are going to work through your house. Using that as your guide, concentrate only on de-cluttering the area shown in each picture, one by one. If you did a thorough job of taking those pictures in the first place, when you reach the end of them, you should be at the end of your house as well. Then you can sit back and enjoy the forest *and* the trees...not to mention the living room.

Exploring the Possibility of Contributing Factors

There's no denying that sometimes the messes in our homes can be greatly exacerbated by issues of a physiological and/or psychological nature. Following are several such issues you may want to consider as you attempt to get your own house in order.

Factor 1

Read the following list of questions and count how many "yeses" and "nos" apply to you.

Question	Circle One	
Does clutter prevent you from living the life you want to live?	Y	N

Do you struggle to stay on top of the papers that come into your home, such as the mail, papers from your kids, papers from work, etc.?	Y	N
Do you have trouble managing money?	Y	N
If you are in charge of food preparation for your family, does the planning/shopping/cooking of all that food often feel like an overwhelming or monumental task, one that makes you weary just to think about?	Y	N
Are problems with paper, money, time, or clutter preventing you from achieving your other goals in life?	Y	N
Do you waste a lot of time trying to find items that have been misplaced?	Y	N
Do you frequently miss important events or deadlines, whether because of something you lost or forgot, because of procrastination, because you underestimated how long it would take to do it, or because you didn't properly break the task down into doable pieces?	Y	N
Do you have trouble calculating time? For example, estimating how long it will take to get to an appointment or how much time you'll need to perform a certain task?	Y	N
Do you have great ideas but often have trouble seeing them through?	Y	N

Do you get lost for hours at a time in tasks you love doing, such as reading or writing or cooking or painting?	Y	N
Are you better at starting things than finishing them?	Y	N
Do people praise your potential more than your accomplishments?	Y	N
Do you feel overwhelmed by sounds/smells/busy-ness/conversations around you? For example, do you have trouble shopping in a store where the music is too loud?	Y	N
Do you often awake determined that this is the day you'll finally get a handle on things, only to feel by the end of the day as if you have failed, yet again, to do so?	Y	N
Do you tend to jump into things too fully with too much enthusiasm and then burn out before they are finished?	Y	N
Do you find yourself apologizing all too frequently for not returning calls/sending thank-you notes/giving gifts in a timely manner?	Y	N
Do you seem to spend more time than the average person daydreaming, being creative, imagining things, and self-talking? Similarly, have you often been called an "airhead" or a "space cadet," either now or when you were younger?	Y	N

Have you always been the type of person who often forgets what you were just in the middle of doing? For example, you walk into a room and you don't know why you're there, or in the middle of a shower you can't recall whether or not you've already shampooed your hair? (As this sort of thing can be part of the normal process of aging, circle Y only if you have always been this way, not if this is a more recent development. If this is a newer behavior only, circle N.)	Y	N
Do the people in your life, especially a spouse or children, frequently indicate frustration with how poorly you manage life tasks such as organization, cleaning, or time management?	Y	N
Do friends or family members frequently tell you that you need more self-discipline?	Y	N
At the end of the day, do you consistently lament all the things you didn't get done, things you really intended to but didn't have time to get to?	Y	N
Do you look at other people who cope better/live better/are more organized/are more punctual than you and wonder how they do it?	Y	N
Do you often feel as though your life is out of control?	Y	N
Total _____Y _____N		

If you answered yes to ten or more of the above questions, then you may be in for a surprise. Believe it or not, this is a do-it-yourself symptom checklist to see if you might have ADD. Yes, I'm talking about attention deficit disorder.

Before you scoff and skip over to the next section, hear me out. ADD is a very common cause of chaos and disorder in the home, yet it is a very misunderstood and frequently overlooked condition, thanks to several pervasive myths.

Myth 1: I can't have ADD because I'm able to focus deeply for extended periods of time.

Truth: One of the primary symptoms of ADD is hyperfocus, the ability to zone in on something almost to the exclusion of all else, sometimes for hours or even days at a time. Hyperfocus is often how books get written and houses get designed and inventions get off the ground, but it's also how a lot of people rule out ADD, never realizing that attention deficit and an inability to focus are not the same thing at all. Many successful authors and architects and inventors are successful in part *because* of their ADD and this unique component of the disorder called hyperfocus.

Myth 2: I can't have ADD because I'm not hyperactive. If anything, I'm sort of mellow and slow paced.

Truth: A person can have ADHD, attention deficit hyperactivity disorder, or they can have ADD, attention deficit disorder, which is a very similar disorder but without the hyperactive component. Most of the ADDers I know are low-key, daydreamy-type folks without a hyperactive bone in their bodies.

Myth 3: This can't be ADD because I've always been this way. It must just be my personality or something.

Truth: One of the primary diagnostic criteria for ADD is that such behaviors have been present for many years, usually since childhood. If you gave ten or more "yeses" to the above questions, and if those yeses would apply not just to now but to most of your life, then this is definitely a topic you need to explore further.

A diagnosis of ADD may sound troubling, but in fact it can be a huge relief for many and the beginning of a whole new journey for you. Imagine finding the solution to problems that have plagued you for years. Proper diagnosis and treatment of ADD can be a huge piece of the clean-house puzzle and go a long way toward helping you get a handle on all sorts of skills that you've spent a lifetime thinking were beyond your grasp.

So what now? If your score warrants further attention, here are my suggestions:

1. Visit www.additudemag.com and explore the many wonderful resources offered there. Learn more about the condition and how to pursue an accurate diagnosis.

2. Make an appointment with your regular physician. He or she may handle diagnosis and treatment or may refer you to a specialist, such as a neurologist or psychiatrist, instead.

3. Before you go to your appointment, try out a few online assessment tests for ADD, especially the kind that help indicate the specific type of ADD you may have. These tests are *never* definitive, but if you get the same results from several completely different sources, they may serve as helpful diagnostic tools for your physician. Print off your score sheets and take them along with you to your appointment.

4. Once you have been given a diagnosis, if you really do have ADD, educate yourself about the condition. The best treatment approach is multifaceted and will combine such elements as medication, exercise, behavioral therapy, dietary adjustments, nutritional supplements, and more.

5. Embrace the positives of the condition. You may be deficient at certain basic life skills, but chances are you're also creative, spontaneous, likeable, fun, funny, and a true delight to be around. God made you the way you are for a reason, and as long as you take responsibility for the ways you are hindered by your ADD, you should also celebrate the ways you are blessed by it as well.

Factor 2

Read the following list of questions and count how many "yeses" and "nos" apply to you.

Question	Circle One	
Do you have way too much stuff?	Y	N
Do you find deep satisfaction in acquiring new things, especially things that are free, even if you don't necessarily need them?	Y	N
Do you find it painful to part with your possessions, even items that others do not consider valuable?	Y	N
Has clutter overtaken your living spaces, for example forcing you to eat somewhere other than at a table or covering at least part of the bed where you sleep?	Y	N
Has the amount of clutter in your house had an impact on you socially, for example causing conflict with family members or preventing you from inviting others into your home?	Y	N

Has the amount of clutter in your house caused conflict with neighbors, social service agencies, or landlords?	Y	N

Total _____ Y _____ N

If you answered yes to at least three of the above questions, you may have a problem with hoarding, an issue often associated with obsessive-compulsive disorder. At least you're not alone. There are approximately 1.5 million Americans who are currently suffering from compulsive hoarding.[1]

Hoarding is defined by the specific behaviors of acquiring too much and discarding too little (even items that most people would consider useless) to the extent that such behavior interferes with normal functioning. There are three chief components to compulsive hoarding, including: enormous emotional difficulty in getting rid of things, compulsive acquiring of items (purchased and/or free), and a high level of disorganization and clutter in the home.[2]

So what now? If your score warrants further attention, seek help from a medical professional. The most common treatment approach is a combination of therapy and medication. Though many in the mental health community are pessimistic about the success of overcoming compulsive hoarding, the condition *can* be conquered with the right approach.

I recently met with Helen Lerner, MD, a physician based in the Philadelphia area who is successfully treating addictive behaviors such as emotional overeating as well as hoarding in a fascinating way. According to Lerner, what she has found is that many times hoarding is rooted in unresolved grief. Dr. Lerner says,

> Time and again, as I work with patients who have hoarding issues, it's not unusual to learn that they suffered some sort of tragic loss in early childhood, such as the death of

a parent or sibling. Unable or unallowed to work through the pain of that loss way back when, they found solace in surrounding themselves with *things* instead. Sadly, years—even decades—later, they continue to anesthetize their original pain in that same way, by substituting the lost human connection with material stuff that cannot die nor desert them.

Dr. Lerner's treatment approach is to focus on the initial loss, using what she calls "kind therapy" to gently guide her patients through a belated grieving process. As they allow themselves to experience, at long last, that deeply buried pain, they eventually come to a place of hope and healing on the other side. As they do, their need to cling to and acquire possessions seems to lessen dramatically.

"Hoarding is a symptom, like a fever," Dr. Lerner says. "A good doctor would never treat just a fever itself and ignore the cause behind it. Cure the pneumonia and the fever goes away. Heal the buried grief, and very often the hoarding goes away too—or at least is diminished by a significant degree."

To learn more about Dr. Lerner's efforts and the amazing progress she is making with this difficult-to-treat disorder, visit the House That Cleans Itself page on my website at www.mindystarnsclark.com.

Other Contributing Factors

Though ADD and hoarding are two of the most common factors that can lead to clutter and chaos in a home, don't forget that there can be other physiological and psychological issues at work here as well. Any of the following conditions can contribute significantly to household disorder, including:

+ thyroid issues

+ chronic fatigue syndrome

+ fibromyalgia and other autoimmune disorders

+ emotional trauma

+ brain injury
+ depression
+ chronic pain
+ grief
+ addictions
+ dementia
+ vitamin deficiencies

If you suspect that any of the above may be contributing to your mess, don't hesitate to bring up the topic with your doctor—and the sooner the better. Over the years I have received more than a few letters from readers whose homes were transformed not just because they implemented the HTCI System, but also because they took my advice, followed their own instincts, and pursued contributing factors until they received the proper treatment and were restored to optimum health.

Our homes may be a mess for a number of reasons, both in and out of our control, but for those factors with a psychological or physiological component, there's no reason to suffer any longer. Help is available, but it's up to you to seek it out. Think of this as just one more step on your journey to having a House That Cleans Itself.

19

Of Marriage and Mess

Be completely humble and gentle;
be patient, bearing with one another in love.
Make every effort to keep the unity of the Spirit
through the bond of peace.

EPHESIANS 4:2-3

There's no doubt about it, household mess is a frequent bone of contention between husbands and wives. That's a simple fact of life. Chapter 10, "Make It a Team Effort," dealt with the rules of thumb for how to come together and solve your basic household issues as a team. But there are messes and then there are *messes*.

These bigger issues are what I call the marital land mines of cleaning—the tougher, touchier problems that require more sensitive and thorough handling. Judging by my reader mail, these are the sorts of problems that can lead couples into the battle zone if they are not careful. In this chapter, I'll deal with the two most common housekeeping issues I see coming between husbands and wives and causing serious rifts. These are:

1. the placement of stuff
2. excessive accumulation of certain kinds of stuff

Each of these problems and their HTCI-friendly solutions will be explained below.

The Placement of Stuff

The single most common housekeeping issue I'm asked about has to do with the placement of stuff—usually *his* stuff put in places where *she* doesn't want it. For example:

- ✦ "He leaves his tools on the counter, even though they belong in the cabinet."
- ✦ "He dumps his shoes in the middle of the floor, even though it drives me crazy."
- ✦ "He ignores his papers and piles of mail but then gets mad if I move them off of the table."

Can there be a meeting of the minds when it comes to our homes and our possessions? Yes, there can! The key is to follow five simple rules I've designed for solving these marriage-busting messes in a constructive, loving, and effective manner.

The Five HTCI Rules of Fair Play for What Goes Where

1. *Initiate a conversation.* In a peaceful moment, sit down and discuss the issue, focusing on the problem of the items in question and *not* on anyone's character or behavior. If things are presented correctly, the situation will be seen as a challenge to be solved rather than a condemnation of habits or a questioning of motivations.

2. *Decide if it's a problem or a preference and then explore extenuating circumstances.* Sometimes there are good, legitimate reasons for where stuff does and does not belong and sometimes it's more a matter of aesthetics. For example, if he leaves his tools out where small children might run into them, it's a *problem*, but if she doesn't like it when he leaves newspapers on the floor around his easy chair, it's a *preference*. When faced with conflicting opinions about the placement of one's stuff, it's important to decide which of these you are dealing with, problem or preference, because even though both issues need to be solved, they require different approaches.

Also, you must consider any extenuating circumstances that may be contributing to the issue or that have prevented other solutions from working in the past. For example, maybe you can't store heavier items on the floor because of a bad back, or your shoe storage area no longer works thanks to the new puppy's tendency to chew leather.

3. *If it's a problem, figure out a solution; if it's a preference, negotiate a decision.* If the issue in question is an actual problem and not just a matter of two different housekeeping styles, then it's time to brainstorm solutions and come up with ideas and alternatives for solving the problem.

If the issue in question is more just a matter of preference, ask yourself if this is something you could let go of and ignore. If not, try for negotiation rather than compromise when you can. With compromise, neither one of you gets exactly what you want, but with negotiation, you each get something you want by giving the other person something he or she wants, making both of you happier in the long run.

4. *Agree on rights.* "Rights" are what I call the rules you each agree to adhere by. For example, you have the right to remove the offending item after a certain period of time, but he has the right to expect that the item will be put in a specific, designated place and not simply shoved aside without intention or thought.

5. *Implement the solution/decision and tweak as needed until it works.* As I've said before, if your husband is a natural problem solver, as many men are, you may find this final step quite gratifying. Trust me, there are few things sexier than a clever hubby intent on getting your house clean and keeping it that way.

Putting the Steps into Action

To show the above steps being put into use, let's go through an example featuring the single most frequent his-stuff-in-her-space problem sent in to me by readers. It seems that in homes across the country, husbands and wives are having more than their fair share of arguments about the quality, quantity, and placement of that daily bane of everyone's existence: paper.

Viola's husband Lyle used to leave papers everywhere, especially all over the kitchen table, which was bad enough, but then he made matters worse by getting upset with her if she moved them. To solve this problem the HTCI Fair Play way, they started with rule 1, *initiate a conversation*. Though this was a hot-button issue for them both, they were determined to keep their cool and work together on this because they knew it was a problem that simply had to be solved. To that end, they began their talk with a quick prayer and a mutual affirmation of love for each other, which put them in the right mood and frame of mind for tackling this issue as a team.

As they moved on to step 2, *decide if it's a problem or a preference and then explore extenuating circumstances,* they both agreed it was a real problem and not just a preference. The problem for him was that important papers were getting lost, including bills that were not getting paid. The problem for her was that places like the kitchen table were to be used for eating and homework and had to be cleared multiple times per day and often sprayed and wiped as well. For her to manage their home, feed their children, and so forth, she needed those papers out of her way.

There were, however, extenuating circumstances to this situation. As it turned out, Lyle was the kind of person who needed visual cues to jog his mental to-do list. Without those papers being out and visible, he couldn't remember what needed doing or when. (I suspect that this, in fact, was what had created his paper problem in the first place.)

Keeping that in mind, they moved on to step 3, *if it's a problem, figure out a solution; if it's a preference, negotiate a decision.* This was where things began to get touchy, so I suggested that they do this step in tandem with step 4, *agree on "rights."* Before they could come up with any solutions, they needed to establish two basic rights, or ground rules:

1. He had the right to put down a piece of paper *in certain areas* and expect her to not move it, toss it, or lose it.

2. She had the right to establish paper-free zones throughout their house.

The key was to do these things in ways that were agreeable to both and that didn't exacerbate the existing problem. Their solution, therefore, needed to address the following:

+ If he accidentally left papers in one of her paper-free zones, there needed to be a specified place where she could put those papers so that they wouldn't get lost or forgotten.

+ If she moved one of his papers from a paper-allowed area, it was her responsibility to track it down, return it to him, and take care of any problems that had been created by what she'd done.

+ Once the papers were no longer spread out all over the house, they were going to have to find some new way to address Lyle's need for visual cues.

Moving along to step 5, *implement the solution/decision and tweak as needed until it works,* the two of them started by going room to room throughout their house to decide where he did and did not have the right to put down papers. In each of those rooms, they also discussed what she would do with any papers he accidentally left in any paper-free zones. The key here was to do this step together and draw boundary lines agreeable to both. Eventually, they chose two rooms downstairs and two rooms upstairs where papers were allowed; she chose a single receptacle downstairs and a single receptacle upstairs where she could place any papers found outside of those designated rooms.

Their only argument was at her insistence that they establish the kitchen table as a paper-free zone. He disagreed so strongly that in the end they found another way to go. Rather than allowing papers on the table at random (his choice) or prohibiting papers at the table entirely (her choice), they met in the middle by choosing an attractive, shallow basket, placing it on the table, and allowing him to fill it with papers. As long as he agreed that the only papers on that table would be *contained within that basket,* she was willing to go along with it.

Once their system was put into place, it required some tweaking. Beacause of his need for visual cues, they ended up instituting a combination of "helps," including a bulletin board in the kitchen where he could tack up the most urgent reminders, a tickler file for bill paying, and a digital calendar for keeping better track of dates and commitments.

The container on the kitchen table had to be tweaked as well. It ended up being too shallow, forcing him to process papers more frequently than he was in the habit of doing. Once he replaced it with a much deeper container, however, he found the pendulum swinging too far in the other direction, with the papers building up to such a great extent that payment deadlines were getting missed. Much like Goldilocks, he thought he needed to find one that was "just right." As it turned out, however, the best and final solution involved bringing Viola into the mix. Realizing that Lyle lacked the skills for sorting and sifting, she offered to do a simple presort of all of his papers, an act that made his paper-processing tasks feel less burdensome and more doable overall.

The final tweak that refined their system was when they came up with a regular paper processing routine, something he had always resisted in the past. Knowing it was important that he choose a day, time, and situation where he found such a task the most agreeable, he decided to aim for Saturday afternoons, especially when Viola was nearby cooking supper. This seemed to work for them both, and it turned what had been a major problem into an area of bonding and growth.

Excessive Accumulation of Certain Kinds of Stuff

The second most common problem I hear about from readers is the battle over excessive accumulation of certain types of items, especially collectables, hobby-related belongings, and what I call "sentimental clutter"—that is, your baby's first shoes, old ticket stubs, or your childhood trophy collection. More often than not, one of you tends to hang on to these types of objects, which drives the other one crazy.

Whenever two people who have differing definitions of "how much is too much" are living in the same household, there's going to be a certain amount of conflict. But for some reason when that excess involves collections, hobbies, or mementos, emotions run higher and conflicts cut deeper.

That's why I've come up with some ground rules for working out your differences on such a touchy topic and achieving a neat home despite this particular issue. For ease of discussion, let's say that you are the husband and your wife tends to accumulate amounts of sentimental clutter. (These rules below, however, will generally apply to dealing with collectibles and hobby-related excess as well.)

The Eight HTCI Rules of Fair Play for Dealing with Excess Sentimental Clutter

1. *Understand who determines "quality."* This is the first and most important rule: It is not your place to put value judgments on the various items your spouse considers important or worth keeping. Her criterion is varied, personal, and may never make sense to you. It shouldn't have to. As adults, we all have the right to say that something is "worth keeping," and that should be that. Just because you don't think so doesn't make it less so to your wife.

2. *Agree that "quantity" is a mutual issue.* While you should never be the one to determine *which* items go and which stay, you do have every right to expect your spouse to limit the total *amount* of what stays. The two of you share a home, which gives you both rights and responsibilities. You have the right not to live amid too much of her clutter, no matter how valuable she says the clutter is. She has the responsibility to make sure you don't suffer needlessly because of mere *things*. You are a person and are more important than any stuff. (I'm sure she knows that. It's just hard to show it when she's feeling challenged over treasured possessions.)

The day she married you, she made a vow to love, honor, and cherish you. More than likely she loves and honors and cherishes you more than she does these things that are coming between you. Let her feel your pain and frustration on the *quantity* (again, *not* the quality, just the quantity) of her accumulated chaos. She needs to understand that if she lived alone she could collect stuff until the cows come home, but because she lives with someone else there is going to have to be compromise in this area, and that compromise is one of quantity.

3. *Agree on a reasonable total.* Decide together what a reasonable total quantity of sentimental objects should be. How much of this sort of thing should anyone reasonably expect to have? It depends on the size of your home and number of occupants, and this may take some calculating and negotiating. The key here is for you not to scoff at her, challenge the various items she loves, or harangue her about how silly it all is. It isn't silly to her, and if you can really embrace that truth, you will free her from having to be so defensive. Then she can be objective and honest in return, and as she takes in factors of space and population, she will probably see the need for a defined spatial limit.

If she's a visual-type person, it may be easiest to express these limits in terms of "containers' worth," even though that's not where all of these items are going to end up in the long run. For example, the two of you may decide she could reasonably keep what would amount to one entire stack, ceiling to floor, of 2' x 3' x 2' bins. If your ceilings are eight feet high, that would give her 48 cubic feet for her collection.

You may agree on more or less than that, depending on other variables. Whatever the specifics, you need to arrive at a number that works for both of you. Once you do, agree that you will never harass her again about what she chooses to keep as long as the total quantity never exceeds the agreed-upon cubic footage allotted.

4. *Decide on a mutually agreeable distribution plan.* Here's another point you'll need to work out: While she has the right to put some of these items on display in your home, you have the right to expect her to limit the total amount that can be displayed at any given time—to be limited to a certain amount of shelf space or other display area.

With the above in mind, then, decide together where some of these items could be placed on display in your home. To keep things from looking too cluttered, try to use a curio cabinet or other display-type furniture, preferably glass covered so there's less accumulation of dust. Limit it to a single piece of furniture, if possible, or perhaps one curio cabinet in a main living area and an additional shelf or two in another room. Once you have determined the total display area(s) allowed, the two of you must agree to the following:

- ✦ She cannot display her sentimental clutter anywhere other than in these designated places.

- ✦ She is welcome to rotate the items in her display(s) as desired.

- ✦ Any extra items not currently on display must be kept in her designated storage containers.

- ✦ The number of items in storage and on display must never total more than the agreed-upon maximum limit.

5. *Bring it all together.* Now that you have a plan, it's time to "merge and purge." Choose a room or area that will become the temporary holding zone and processing area for this stuff, preferably somewhere that won't be in the way but that can be accessed easily, such as a guest room or the corner of a garage. Aim for some place that's generally out of sight if possible, because it's going to get messy for a while.

Next, go all over the house and collect every single item that falls into this category of sentimental clutter and take it to that designated room or area. Gather it all—from shelves, piles, even things stored away in the attic. (Be sure to treat the items with care, wrapping and temporarily boxing those that are breakable.) As the pile mounts, your wife's eyes may very well be opened to the extent of this problem. There's nothing like seeing everything all together in one place to grasp the enormity of what has been accumulated.

Even you may be surprised at the quantity and find yourself becoming angry and frustrated as the pile grows. These emotions are understandable, but I urge you to work through them privately or with a trusted friend, not with your spouse. It isn't easy to live with a person who has this tendency, but it also isn't easy to *be* a person with this tendency. She knows she has been causing you pain with what you see as such needless clutter, but she cannot seem to stop herself. This need to hoard sentimental clutter has psychological roots that are not easily untangled.[1] What she needs most at this point is not condemnation but grace and sympathy. Pray that God would give you a heart filled with both. (See endnote 1 for more information on the root cause and treatment for this problem.)

6. *Winnow it down.* In rule 3 above, the two of you agreed to a container limit. Get those containers now and bring them into this processing area. This next step is for her to narrow down the total amount of items into no more than can fit into the containers. Before she starts, stress this important rule of thumb: *If you can't remember why you saved it, it's not important anymore and needs to go.*

This concept can be tough to grasp, but doing so can help greatly when winnowing down a large collection. The only reason many of these items ever had any importance at all was because of the feelings and memories attached to them. But if the sight of some particular thing no longer brings up any memories or feelings, then its importance has now passed. It's time to release it and move on to something that actually does still bring up special thoughts and feelings.

7. *Be a helpmate.* This winnowing process will probably be difficult, but there are definitely ways a spouse can help, such as:

+ Keep her on track by helping to establish goals and then providing rewards along the way when she meets those goals.

+ If she'd like, keep her company sometimes when she works.

+ Provide mini treats once in a while, such as five minutes of back rubbing for every half hour she spends whittling.

+ Think like a team. Boost your teammate by praising and rewarding her hard-won progress.

✦ Offer to take over some regular chore of hers to free up more time she can spend winnowing.

When she is finished—when she gets the total collection down to what will fit in those designated containers—celebrate. She did it! God bless her, it wasn't easy, but she did it.

8. *Create the display.* Once the collection has been narrowed down into only what will fit in the agreed upon number of containers, and once all excess has been removed from the premises, it is finally time to move on to the fun part: putting a choice of items on display in the designated display areas. Though she may find it frustrating that not everything she owns is allowed to be out at once, she should bear in mind that this concept is not unusual. In fact, it's a guiding principle employed by museums around the world: Some of the collection goes on display, some goes into storage, and once in a while the stock gets rotated. Certainly, the most important items can be assigned a permanent place in your home's display, but for the lesser items, rotate them on a regular basis.

What your own collector may be surprised to find is that some things become even more special to her when they have been tucked away out of sight for a while. The opposite is true is well. For some people, every time they rotate their collection, they find it easier and easier to part with a few more items that no longer seem all that special.

Turnabout Is Fair Play

Several years ago a reader sent me such a heartfelt plea for help with this problem of sentimental clutter that I responded at length, spelling out much of the advice that would eventually form the basis for the above set of rules. She wrote back right away, thanking me for the advice and saying that she and her husband had already started working toward a compromise.

Much to my delight, she followed up a year later with another note to let me know how the process had gone in the long run. To her amazement, she found that once they had set a maximum total limit for his collection, she was no longer upset by it at all. In fact, the sight of it eventually even made her smile.

That news made me so happy because this is exactly what a House That Cleans Itself is all about. The HTCI System has nothing to do with impressing the neighbors with shiny clean floors or passing some fuss-budget's white glove test. It's about solving your messes in such a way that not only does your frustration disappear, but the solutions you and your loved ones have achieved together actually give you joy.

God bless all who attempt to navigate their trickiest marital messes with love and compassion the HTCI way. The journey isn't easy, but it's always worth it in the end!

20

Using the CONVERT System

Whatever you do, work at it with all your heart,
as working for the Lord, not for human masters,
since you know that you will receive an inheritance
from the Lord as a reward.
It is the Lord Christ you are serving.

COLOSSIANS 3:23-24

The original version of this book centered around what I call the CONVERT system, a specific but time-consuming step-by-step approach for turning a messy home into a House That Cleans Itself. After that book came out, the feedback I received from my readers—and my own continued work with the system—led me to see that attaining a House That Cleans Itself is not so much about following a step-by-step conversion as it is about embracing a completely new way of thinking and acting when it comes to one's home and possessions.

In this new-and-improved version of the book, I have chosen to shift the focus to a more flexible approach. If, however, you are the type of person who prefers regimented, step-by-step instruction, I have included a simplified explanation of the original CONVERT system here for your convenience.

The letters of the CONVERT acronym stand for:

C lear out the clutter

O pen up and clean

N eaten, organize, and solve problem spots

V erify rabbit trails and set up stations

E xamine sight zones

R ecord future improvements needed

T ake steps now for ongoing maintenance

But before you can CONVERT, you need to gather evidence as described in chapter 4 of this book, "Become a Detective." Once you've read that chapter and completed those steps, you are ready to continue here.

The CONVERT System

This is a room-by-room and day-by-day conversion process, so prepare for some heavy-duty organizing and cleaning as you embark on this exciting journey. The CONVERT process is straightforward, but you really need to think of your house as "under construction" because it can take a while. Before you get started, here are some basic ground rules:

+ To move through the process in an organized fashion, you should start by sketching a floor plan of your home, then numbering each room in the order you'd like to CONVERT it.

+ As you work through your house, make sure not to spend so much time on any given day or so many days in a row that you burn out before the job is complete. Whether you can put in an hour a day twice a week or five hours a day six days a week, eventually you will make it to the end of this conversion. When you are finished, you will be the proud and much-less-overburdened inhabitant of a House That Cleans Itself. Your efforts will have paid off, and you'll reap the benefits of less stress and more time.

✦ To have the fastest impact on your house, *complete all seven steps of CONVERT in one area before you start the next area.* This may not be the most efficient way to de-clutter or clean, but it is the best way to CONVERT your home to a House That Cleans Itself for four reasons:

1. Once an area is finished, it will stay neater and cleaner and require less time to maintain.

2. You will learn as you go, seeing what really does work and what needs additional tweaking. This will help you do an even better job in subsequent areas.

3. Changing from one task to the next helps you circumvent some of your natural housekeeping "impairments," such as difficulty in making decisions or focusing, by allowing you to do these things in short bursts rather than prolonged agony.

4. The payoff of completion as you finish each area will spur you on. For a project this big, you need payoffs all along the way.

Gather Your Tools

The tools you need for your conversion include:

✦ *Garbage bags, clean trash cans, laundry baskets, boxes, or any other containers that can be used as holders for different items as you work.* Label one container "Yard Sale," another "Donate," another "Other Rooms," or whatever labels best serve your organizing purposes. As you clean, place your things in the correct containers.

✦ *Cleaning supplies.* Yes, it's true that a House That Cleans Itself eliminates much of the daily mopping and wiping

you have to do, but you'll want to include deep cleaning
as a part of the process as you work your way through
the house this first time.

✦ *Sheets or blankets.* As I said before, this process may take
a while, so give yourself a break. On the way to looking
great, your house may look worse than it did before.
Remember to take your emotions out of your cleaning,
don't blame yourself for the condition it's in, and instead
commend yourself for CONVERTing. When you've finished each day, drape the blankets or sheets over the
boxes and bags and proclaim that what's underneath is
off limits for now. This will keep things looking as neat
as possible and keep everyone from rummaging through
the items to save them or move them.

Getting Started

Once you're ready to begin, grab your tools, take a look at the floor
plan of your house, and head to the room you designated with the number 1. Working through the letters of CONVERT, it's time to:

Clear out the clutter. Start by attacking the visible items on counters
and tables and then move on to drawers, containers, cabinets, and closets. Purge as much as you can, giving away or throwing away. Remember to place in your designated bins all items that don't belong in this
room. After the clutter has been completely cleared from this entire
area, move out the bags of donations and trash, put your sorting cans
and boxes into area number 2 on your schedule, drape the blanket over
them, and then return to this area. (For more information about de-
cluttering, read chapter 8, "Aim for Simplicity.")

Open up and clean. Use your deep-cleaning tools for vacuuming,
dusting, wiping, and mopping the entire area you have just de-cluttered.

Neaten, organize, and solve problem spots. Using your evidence record,
review the list you made of messes in this room and their root causes,
and then implement creative problem solving to eliminate those causes.

(For more information about creative problem solving, read chapter 5, "Change the House to Fit the Behavior.")

Verify and set up stations as needed. If any stations will be located in this room, this is the time to assemble those and put them in place. (For more information about setting up stations, read chapter 7, "Think like a Hotel," and chapter 13, "Sample Stations.")

Examine sight zones. Now that the room has been purged, cleaned, neatened, and problem solved, stand in the doorway and make sure the sight zone is neat and attractive and that it has a focal point. Fix any problems you notice. (For more information about working with sight zones, read chapter 6, "Create a First Impression of Clean.")

Record future improvements needed. Make note of any maintenance issues that need to be addressed in this area, as well as any larger changes you want to consider for upgrading this space in the future.

Take steps now for ongoing maintenance. Make a mental note of how this room looks now and what items belong in this space. Verify that there is a trash can in this room or next door. Set up a small quick clean station with the appropriate tools needed to keep this space neat and clean. (For more information about ongoing maintenance, read chapter 12, "Maintaining Your Achievement.")

Once you have finished the above steps, area 1 has now successfully been CONVERTed. Congratulations!

Now you can move along to room 2 and repeat the CONVERT steps for that area. Continue to do this throughout your home until your conversion is complete.

Then sit back, relax, and see just how great it is to live in a House That Cleans Itself!

My Most Embarrassing Messy House Story
—A Better Mousetrap—
BY JESSIE R.

Living in a farmhouse, we have mice. Lots of them. Even though our cat is an excellent mouser, she still misses a few here and there. One of them set up shop in the oven. I decided to try the new mousetraps, which are basically a tray of adhesive. Because I suspected the mouse had invited friends, I got the rat-sized one. I caught a couple in the first trap. Giddy with success, I put a second one in the oven.

Unfortunately, I later forgot about it and turned the oven on to preheat. The adhesive bubbled over, the tray melted, the house filled with fumes, the smoke detector wouldn't quit, and we had to open all the doors and windows and have a picnic supper that night. When the oven cooled off, I had to scrape the adhesive off the bottom with a putty knife.

At least the trap had been empty when I did it. I shudder to think what it would have been like to clean up all that mess—and roasted mouse too.

21

Cleaning a House That Cleans Itself

The Spirit God gave us does not make us timid,
but gives us power, love and self-discipline.

2 TIMOTHY 1:7

All houses get dirty and need cleaning. That's a fact of life. The good news is that many of the House That Cleans Itself techniques described throughout this book will reduce the quantity of dirt in your home and the frequency with which you'll need to do actual cleaning. This chapter shows you how to clean a House That Cleans Itself, offering various tips and techniques especially effective for the housekeeping impaired.

No More All-or-Nothing

From the mud we track in to the skin we slough off, we humans can't escape the basic truth that life is messy. If you are housekeeping impaired, chances are you think of cleaning as an isolated event you do periodically in an all-or-nothing fashion.

In fact, cleaning is not supposed to be like that. It's not something you do once a week for two hours or once every two weeks for five. In a House That Cleans Itself, *cleaning is an activity that must be integrated into your everyday life*, just like brushing your teeth or taking your medicine. Cleaning may not be tons of fun, but it doesn't have to be that big of a deal either. In most cases, the HTCI System is about changing your house rather than your behavior, but in this area, your behavior must change as well.

Much of my personal housekeeping battle came to an end when I finally surrendered my all-or-nothing tendency and decided I didn't want to be that way anymore. I reframed my concept of what cleaning means and set up three different stations to reflect this new way of thinking:

1. *Quick clean station*—to be used frequently to wipe up small messes, such as crumbs, smears, and fingerprints

2. *Intermediate clean station*—also to be used frequently to clean up small messes that require larger tools that can't be duplicated in every room, such as a rechargeable vacuum and an instant mop

3. *Deep clean station*—to be used for the regular, more involved cleaning that every house requires on a periodic basis

Each of these is described below.

Quick Clean Station

A quick clean station is exactly what the name implies. It is a collection of cleaning products and supplies gathered together in a single container and placed in a convenient location so you can quickly and easily get rid of messes in that location. *Almost every one of the rooms in your house should have its own quick clean station.* In many cases the station will consist of nothing more than a pack of disposable wipes.

Can you imagine what would happen if you put an assortment of disposable wipes in nearly every room of your house? Do you think you might be more likely to give the dirty bathroom counter a swipe if all you had to do was reach into the medicine cabinet and pull out a wipe? How easy it is to clean the front window when a pack of window-cleaning wipes is tucked in the nearest drawer. To the housekeeping impaired, disposable wipes can be one of the most useful tools you will ever have at your fingertips. Buy them and use them. They are wonderful.

Quick clean stations should contain wipes appropriate for each surface in that room. For example, if you have a ceramic, glass, or porcelain cooktop, you should have a pack of stove top wipes stored nearby. The ones I prefer are smooth on one side and safely abrasive on the other, which makes them handy for scrubbing burned-on messes without harming the finish. In the bathroom you might have antibacterial wipes for the counter, sink, toilet, and bath, and glass wipes for the mirror and window. For the living room, you may include electronic wipes for the stereo components and dusting wipes for wood furniture. (Though you should avoid using any chemicals on your finest wood.)

Intermediate Clean Station

Some of the messes you come across are going to require bigger tools, such as a mop or vacuum cleaner, but you can't have one of these in every room. You can, however, have these intermediate level cleaning tools for each of the major sections of your home. For example, you might have one set upstairs and one set downstairs. Your intermediate level tools include:

+ a rechargeable, battery-operated vacuum cleaner
+ an automatic mop, such as a Swiffer WetJet
+ an extendable ostrich-feather duster

By making these cleaning tools convenient to the part of the house you're in, you are much more likely to grab and use them when you spot a mess. More importantly, your kids will too, although they may need to be reminded now and then.

Deep Clean Station

Somewhere in your home you must establish a place for all those other cleaning tools (including the heavy-duty versions of the intermediate-level tools). From silver polish to oven cleaner, paper towels to rubber gloves, the items you need to get your house fully and deeply clean should be accessible, organized, and uncluttered. Did you know that cleaners can cause clutter? Take a look in your cleaning closet. Toss all out-of-date items as well as any you never use. Just because that expanding dryer-lint-hose-wiper was a good idea when you bought it doesn't mean you'll ever get around to using it again. Does it really deserve to take up three square feet of prime closet space?

Once you have purged all but the essentials from your deep clean station, look at what's left. Are any important tools or products missing? Think in terms of supplies for the following:

+ *general surfaces* (spray cleaners, sponges, and rags)
+ *specialized surfaces* (wood polish and oven cleaner)
+ *floors* (broom, mop and extra mop heads, bucket, floor cleaner, and vacuum cleaner with extra attachments and bags)
+ *trash* (trash bags and string for recycling newspapers)

How you organize your cleaners depends on the space you are working with. I keep my cleaners inside a closet on a metal shelving unit. My friend Sue has most of hers hanging from hooks on a pegboard in her laundry room. Whatever system you use, make sure your deep clean station has everything you really need and nothing you don't.

Once you've established the three cleaning stations—quick, intermediate, and deep—it's time to put them to use and keep your clean home sparkling for good.

Learning to Quick Clean

How long do you think it takes to unload the dishwasher? Fold a load of laundry? Clean a toilet? If you are housekeeping impaired, chances are you grossly overestimate the time needed for many household tasks. Working at a normal speed, these three jobs take about three minutes each.

How about wiping fingerprints from the front of the refrigerator? Changing out dirty towels for clean ones in the bathroom? Dusting a ceiling fan?

If your home is set up with easily accessible cleaning tools, each of these jobs requires less than a minute and sometimes as little as 30 seconds. If you think about the number of times in any given day you have anywhere from 30 seconds to 4 minutes to spare, you'll grasp the importance of this concept: Quick cleaning is the single best way to stay on top of household messes.

Let's take a look at time. Think of the things you do in a day that require waiting on:

+ a frozen dinner cooking in the microwave

+ the school bus to come

+ the dog to come inside

+ your kids to finish brushing their teeth so you can tuck them in

+ the water in the shower to heat up

In terms of tiny segments of time, it's quite possible to teach yourself to match brief opportunities of "waiting time" with "just as briefly accomplished" cleaning tasks. For example, it takes me about three minutes to unload my dishwasher. It also takes three minutes to cook my favorite frozen meal for lunch. Whenever I start the microwave for three minutes, I make myself load or unload the dishwasher as my meal is cooking.

To the average person this is a no-brainer. But to the housekeeping impaired, it feels strange indeed. In the past I would have spent those three minutes frittering around the kitchen, maybe flipping through a pile of mail, glancing at a magazine, checking my voice mail, or even just standing there channel-flipping on the kitchen television. Why wouldn't I have spent that time cleaning? As the housekeeping impaired person might say,

+ "I'm already busy cooking, and I can't clean if I'm already doing something else."

+ "This isn't my cleaning time. I only clean when I have the time to do it right and do it completely."

+ "It never crossed my mind."

+ "I didn't even notice it needed doing."

There are plenty of reasons some folks don't naturally seize random moments available to them throughout the day and use those for cleaning. *But in a House That Cleans Itself, random moments of brief cleaning are a vital part of what keeps the house clean.* We just have to teach ourselves to take advantage of the time that comes our way.

Create a Quick Clean Guide

The first step in training yourself to quick clean is to make a list of various individual cleaning tasks and the time it takes to complete them. To that end, grab pen and paper and a stopwatch or a watch with a second hand. You can do this by yourself, but it's also a fun activity with children. For younger children, they can yell "Go!" and press the start button; for older children, you can take turns timing each other.

Whether working alone or accompanied, choose some common tasks you think might qualify as "quick cleaning" for a given area. In a front entryway, these may include:

+ wiping down the door and door frame

+ shaking dirt out of the floor mat

+ cleaning the glass with glass-cleaning wipes

+ dusting furniture with dusting wipes

+ watering plants

+ dusting the light fixture

+ sweeping and mopping up tracked-in dirt

Write down a task, and then do the following:

+ Stand in the middle of the room.

+ Start the timer.

+ Retrieve the product(s) needed to do that task. Most products should be in your quick clean or intermediate clean stations, though you may also need to do things like get a cup of water from the kitchen to water a plant or grab a pair of shoes to go outside to shake out a dirty floor mat.

This is not a race. Move no more quickly or slowly than you would on any given day as you would normally perform this task.

When you're finished:

+ Put away your cleaning tools.

+ Throw away any trash you've generated, such as dirty wipes.

+ Return to the middle of the room.

+ Stop the timer.

Now write down how long that task took. Repeat the above steps for various common tasks, keeping a list as you go. When you are finished, your list may look like this:

+ wiping down the door and door frame—30 seconds

+ shaking dirt out of the floor mat—1 minute, 6 seconds

+ cleaning the glass with glass-cleaning wipes—42 seconds

+ dusting furniture with dusting wipes—1 minute, 12 seconds

+ watering plants—45 seconds

+ dusting the light fixture—18 seconds

+ sweeping and mopping up tracked-in dirt—2 minutes, 15 seconds

You may be surprised at how quickly most of these tasks can be accomplished, which is good because that's the point. By taking a vague all-or-nothing concept like "clean the house" and turning it into much smaller, more specific tasks with times assigned, such as an 18-second action of retrieving the long-handled duster, running it over the light fixture, and returning the duster to the closet, you make quick cleaning a painless, nonintimidating prospect that can be done in stolen moments during the day.

Consider posting this list somewhere in the area, perhaps on the inside of a cabinet door, and then make more such lists for other rooms in your house. Then, if you regularly wait for something in a certain room or area, pass through it at certain times of the day, or even make it part of a first-thing-in-the-morning or last-thing-in-the-evening routine, try to associate what you're doing with a cleaning task. Before you know it, the act of brushing your teeth will remind you to wipe down the bathroom counter, getting up in the morning will include making your bed, and waiting to tuck in your kids at night can mean a quick straightening of the sheets and towels in the linen closet.

At the very least, whenever you find yourself with a few extra minutes, pick one or two quick clean tasks that will fit your time. That way, even if you only have "two minutes to spare," as we so often do, you can use those minutes efficiently and easily by letting the list be your guide.

Remember too that this list isn't just for you. It's for *every* person who lives in your house who is old enough and capable enough to clean. Train everyone to utilize the list throughout the day. You'll soon be amazed at how many messes disappear. For younger children, get them started in this practice by making a second list tailored just for them. Snap some photos of them doing specific tasks, such as putting away their bathtub toys or wiping the lower cabinets with a wet washcloth. Put the photos on the fridge—and don't forget to praise your kids for their work. Train up those kids in the way they should go, and when they are grown, they won't be housekeeping impaired!

For older children and teens who aren't accustomed to thinking about cleaning at all, I suggest you give them tasks in a given area that relates to a specific part of their day. For example, if your daughter likes to spend time on Facebook, make her the official cleaner of the computer area. Stash a packet of wipes within easy reach and remind her to use them when she's online. If your son enjoys playing basketball in the driveway, make it his job to sweep the front walk when he goes out to play.

Learning to Deep Clean

No matter how much we don't want to think about it, now and then every house needs more than just a quick clean—even a House That Cleans Itself. Deep cleaning may never be your forte, but at least there's a huge difference between deep cleaning a regular house and a House That Cleans Itself. Why? Because in the past much of your cleaning time wasn't spent cleaning at all. It was spent neatening, shuffling clutter, and gathering your cleaning supplies. Imagine setting out to deep clean with easy-to-find tools in an already neat house. Is that a radical thought? For the housekeeping impaired, it might have been before, but not any longer. Get ready to live the way those "other" people live, where deep cleaning is a normal weekly task that requires no more or less effort than it ought to.

There are many different approaches to take with the who's, how's, and when's of deep cleaning. After much research and trial and error, I have settled upon three favorite methods for the housekeeping impaired to handle the deep cleaning. I suggest you try all three to find out which one is the most successful for you and your family members:

1. *Room ownership*—this is best for a home whose room count is no more than twice the number of people who live there (that is, a single person with a two-room apartment, a family of three with a six-room house, and so on).

2. *Day division*—this is best for singles and smaller families.

3. *Room-to-room sequencing*—this is good for a home with at least four capable family members (such as two adults and two teens), though it can include younger family members as well.

Each of these methods is explained below.

Room Ownership

When my kids were younger, the hardest part of getting them to help around the house was the blame game. For every five things I told them to pick up or put away, three of those had nothing to do with them, so they balked when told to clean. "But *she* left it there. Tell *her* to clean it!" "That mess is *hers,* not mine!" On and on it went.

Yes, we had a few lessons about the basic family dynamic of "all for one and one for all," but still I had to admit there was a certain logic to their complaints. If they were both in a room when it got messy but one simply dropped a few books on the floor and the other left out a bunch of dirty plates and spilled cracker crumbs from one end of the couch to the other, where was the fairness in giving them an equal load in cleaning?

On the other hand, why should I have to be the one to divide out and enforce individual responsibility? I just wanted the room clean regardless of who messed it up. The blame game used to make me nuts.

Then I came up with the room ownership principle. In room ownership, the various common rooms of the house are assigned to different family members. It is their job to see that the room stays neat during the week and gets its deep cleaning at the end of the week. That's a fairly common division of responsibility for big families, but here is our twist: The person who owned that room was not necessarily required to clean everything in that room but merely held the chief responsibility of seeing that it got cleaned. Therefore, if big sister owns the family room but little sister made a big mess in there, it's big sister's job to go and get little sister and have her clean up the mess she made.

It sounds simple, but this method does more than just get rooms clean. It takes the parents out of the roll of arbiter and enforcer; it slowly teaches kids to be more considerate of other people's spaces; it allows people to become familiar with the responsibilities of getting specific and limited areas clean, thus making them more efficient; and it tends to give the owners a certain sense of pride in the rooms, which makes them more likely to keep them clean.

There are a few basic rules for room ownership:

+ If someone has made a mess in your room, you may go get him and have him clean up that mess, but you must not do it in a disrespectful manner. You may also choose to give him a break and simply clean his mess yourself. It's your choice, but it must be done without resentment or sharp words.

+ If someone comes and gets you and says you left a mess in her room, you must stop what you're doing if at all possible and go and fix the mess you made in her room.

+ Rooms should be assigned based on age and ability. In our house, I usually took the kitchen and dining room, Dad handled the exterior yard and structures and cars, and our two daughters divided out the family room, bathrooms, entryway, and hallways.

+ If younger children are in the house, they can be assigned as a "room buddy" and given simple tasks. Even a toddler knows when he is part of the family cleaning routine. He can help by dusting the baseboards and lower cabinets with a dry rag. (He might miss a few spots, but he's sure building a great habit.)

+ Each person is responsible for organizing and replenishing the cleaning tools needed for their room. (Requests for cleaning products can be written on a master shopping list on the fridge.) To help build enthusiasm, each person should be allowed to buy a cleaning-tool carrier of his choice for storing his tools. He may want a bright-red plastic bin, a handled caddy, or even a carpenter's apron. (A kid in a carpenter's apron that has been fully stocked with spray cleaners, paper towels, and rags is a force to be reckoned with and a great soldier in the battle against grime.)

✦ To prevent conflicts over sharing vacuum cleaners, mops, and so forth, general times or days for use should be assigned in a staggered fashion.

What deep cleaning tasks should be done in each room? In general, once a week or at least once every other week, the rooms should be cleaned as follows:

family room

✦ clean in or around fireplace as needed
✦ dust all furniture
✦ clean all glass and metal
✦ vacuum floors and all upholstered furniture
✦ vacuum or run duster high along the walls and around the rim of the ceiling
✦ mop any hardwood floors
✦ neatly arrange couch pillows, cushions, and knickknacks
✦ empty trash

kitchen

✦ disinfect countertops, backsplash, table, stove
✦ wipe all large appliances and small appliances
✦ wipe all cabinet fronts and knobs
✦ wipe around doorways, light switches, air vents
✦ vacuum floor
✦ mop floor
✦ dry out sink
✦ toss old food from fridge
✦ wipe down inside of fridge
✦ wipe stove vent
✦ wipe out the inside of the microwave

bedrooms

+ strip linens and take to laundry room

+ put on clean linens and make bed

+ take dirty clothes to laundry room

+ dust all furniture

+ clean all visible glass, such as mirrors and prominent windows

+ vacuum carpets

+ mop hardwood floors

+ vacuum underneath the bed and in the floors of closets

+ dust tops of wood moldings around windows and doors

bathrooms

+ spray and wipe toilet and toilet bowl

+ spray and wipe sink and base

+ spray and wipe tub and shower

+ clean all glass and metal

+ wipe walls around sink area, toilet area, and bath area

+ vacuum floor

+ mop the floor with disinfectant

+ hang fresh towels and take dirty ones to laundry room

+ replenish toilet paper as needed

+ straighten magazines, shelves, and so forth as needed

other areas

+ neatening

+ dusting

+ glass, metal, and electronics cleaning

+ vacuuming

- mopping

About once a month, you should:

- wipe the top of the fridge
- clean the less visible windows
- dust all lampshades and ceiling fans

About once every three months, you should:

- wash comforters, bedspreads, and pillows
- clear out and clean under the bathroom sink
- clean out the medicine cabinet
- dust all mini blinds
- clean the most visible windows inside and out

About every six months, you should

- wash curtains
- air out house
- have rugs cleaned
- hose down the front porch, house exterior, and garage door
- clean the less visible windows inside and out

If you choose the room ownership method for deep cleaning, make sure you make a list of the tasks required for each room. Go over the list with each owner to make sure the person understands how to do all jobs. For consistency, advise your cleaners always to work from left to right and top to bottom, just like the housecleaning experts do.

With the room ownership method, it's important to find a fun but fair way to choose who gets what room. Different family members will often gravitate toward different room choices on their own, but if the division doesn't happen naturally, make it a game to decide who will be doing what. Buy as many candy bars (or something more healthful if you prefer) as there are rooms and write on the back of each bar the name of a room. Spread out the bars on a table and let everyone pick two. They get to keep the candy and those rooms. Swaps are allowed when mutually agreeable.

Finally, put a time limit on room ownership, usually one month, so that no one is stuck with the more difficult rooms for long. This way every family member eventually has a chance to learn how to clean each room in the house.

Day Division

Day division is a good choice for cleaning when the bulk of the work falls to one or two people, especially if those people are quite busy with other parts of their lives. With day division, there is no single day of deep cleaning. Instead, the cleaning is divided into six separate chunks, each of which is accomplished on a different day of the week.

There is nothing new about this system. Having a specific "laundry day," for example, probably started when Adam and Eve traded in their fig leaves for animal skins. Nowadays, day division cleaning may appeal to you if you work at a job all week and don't want to sacrifice the bulk of your day off to getting your house under control.

To set up your own day division system, write down in broad terms the tasks required to deep clean your house, such as vacuuming; mopping; dusting; glass cleaning; horizontal wiping with cloth and cleaner; vertical wiping with cloth and cleaner; laundry; cleaning out the fridge; cleaning toilets, tubs, and showers; sweeping exteriors; cleaning windows; emptying trash.

In your notebook draw six columns and label them with the days of the week, Monday through Saturday. Looking at your list of tasks, assign the more obvious ones where they would fall. For example, if you like to cook on Fridays, put cooking there—and make a week's worth of meals on that single day. If you like to start the week with clean laundry, make Saturday your laundry day. When you are finished giving each day a task, your chart might look like this:

Monday	Tuesday	Wednesday	Thursday	Friday	Saturday
tubs & toilets	dust & glass	vert. wiping	mop	cooking	laundry
trash	horiz. wiping	vacuum	trash	clean fridge	exteriors
			grocery shop	clean stove	cars

Make sure that certain tasks precede others. For example, you want to wipe and dust prior to vacuuming, and you want to vacuum prior to mopping.

This system may or may not appeal to you. For some, it's such a relief to avoid a single big three- or four-hour cleaning day that cleaning a little bit each day is better. For others, spreading the job out like this makes them feel as though they are always cleaning, so it doesn't work as well. (For me, the biggest drawback of this method is that when my family does it this way, we don't get that "deep clean euphoria" payoff that comes when strolling through a spotless house after several concentrated hours of hard work.)

If you decide to try the day division method of cleaning, tweak your list on a weekly basis until you feel it is working best for you. (For example, if you usually work late on Wednesdays, move one of those tasks to Tuesdays and the other to Thursdays.) You might also consider using this system every *other* week rather than weekly if your home doesn't get that dirty in between cleanings.

Day division cleaning is worth trying for a month or so. If you find that having a short, daily deep cleaning session feels like less work than a longer, single, weekly deep cleaning session would, this is probably the best plan for you.

Room-to-Room Sequencing

When our kids were teenagers, room-to-room sequencing was our cleaning method of choice. It worked for us because our children were old enough to handle any cleaning task our house required. It was especially good for those of us who tended to drag on too long with certain cleaning tasks or get sidetracked while cleaning. Some other big plusses for this system are:

+ The work moves very quickly because there's a certain urgency that comes from being followed.

+ No one feels as though he or she is getting a bum rap because everyone works equally hard.

+ It truly makes you feel like a team eagerly striving toward a common goal.

A big minus of this system is that it can take longer to get set up and rolling in the beginning. I was shocked to find it took me an entire day to go from room to room in my house writing down all necessary cleaning tasks in specific detail, and then charting out what each person's responsibilities were for each room. It was like working out the pieces of a big puzzle. When it finally came together, though, it did so beautifully. Here's how it's done.

Each person is assigned a number and several primary tasks, for example:

+ Dad—neatener, preparer, high duster

+ Mom—wiper, disinfectant sprayer, tub scrubber

+ Teen A—vacuumer, toilet cleaner

+ Teen B—mopper, finisher

Next, each person is given a list of rooms in a specific order and the tasks they are to complete in each room. At the words "Let's go," each person takes his list in hand and begins to work through it. The lists are carefully coordinated so there are no traffic jams, and everyone is making a full sweep around the house in a very specific sequence.

For example, while person 1 is gathering supplies from the cleaning closet, person 2 is stripping the sheets from all of the beds, person 3 is doing the dishes, and person 4 is gathering up the dirty laundry in the house and carrying it to the laundry room. When person 1 has his supplies, he moves into the first room and begins his share of the cleaning:

+ Straightening up any mess, putting anything that belongs elsewhere in a laundry basket for redistributing.

+ Preparing the room for the vacuumer and mopper by clearing the way—removing knickknacks and other items from tables and desks and picking up smaller things from the floor, such as baskets or floor mats (each room should have a prearranged place for those items to be clustered temporarily, such as on the couch or a chair).

+ Running an extended-reach ostrich feather duster along the tops of cabinets, high shelves, upper walls, and ceiling.

When he is finished with those three tasks, he calls out "Done!" and moves into the next room, where he does the same basic actions again. He will proceed throughout the house, attacking each new space in order as the neatener, preparer, and high duster.

Meanwhile, as soon as person 1 finishes in a room and shouts that he is done, person 2 moves right into that room and starts her work. As the designated wiper, disinfectant sprayer, and tub scrubber, she will be dusting and wiping all surfaces, cleaning all glass, and scrubbing all showers and tubs as she comes to them.

As soon as she is finished with a room, she moves on to the next one, and person 3 takes her place. As the vacuumer and toilet cleaner, her job is fairly straightforward.

Finally, when person 3 is ready to move on, person 4 goes to that room and starts her work. Number 4's tasks include "finishing"—putting back all the things that person 1 moved off of tables and counters, such as knickknacks and baskets, replacing hand towels where needed, replenishing toilet paper and tissues, and so forth. Once the space looks lovely and is completely put back together, she dumps the trash into a big bag she carries with her, mops the floor, and turns off the light.

As you can see by now, what's happening throughout the house is that each room is getting cleaned by four different people, one at a time, in a row, with each person doing different tasks. By the time person 4 moves into the second room to repeat her tasks there, person 3 is working in the third room, person 2 is in the fourth room, and person

1 is in the fifth room. This sort of room-by-room sequencing continues throughout the house until the entire place sparkles from top to bottom.

This system seems the most complicated on paper, but once it is put into action it becomes much simpler. The hardest part is timing tasks to prevent traffic jams. That is best done by observing where those jams tend to happen (as in person 1 is still doing his job in the kitchen when person 2 moves in and starts her job, and she is quickly followed by person 3, who is ready to do her job but can't because 1 and 2 are in her way). This happens because not every task takes as long in every room. Where the wiper might spend half an hour wiping down the cabinets, appliances, and counters in the kitchen, the vacuumer may only need 10 minutes in there. In the living room, on the other hand, the vacuumer may spend 20 minutes vacuuming pet hair from a difficult rug while the wiper just has to dust a few tables and breeze on through.

To prevent traffic jams, once you see when and where they happen, tweak each person's task list to slow them down or speed them up accordingly. For example, at the point where the mopper usually catches up with the vacuumer, her task list might say, "Check out back to see that the patio furniture is neat, the yard looks good, and sweep the deck." By the time she has done those tasks and comes back inside, there is no longer a backlog because the person ahead of her has finished and moved on.

If room-to-room sequence cleaning appeals to you, give it a try! Like a giant wave, it will wash through your entire house, leaving cleanliness in its wake. To motivate our teenagers, we agreed to take the money we would be saving on a housekeeper and apply it toward a big family trip. In our area, the going rate for housecleaners is around $100 per visit, so as you can imagine the savings piled up rather quickly. A year later we were headed to Hawaii, where we gladly didn't have to clean a thing—except the sand from the soles of our feet.

My Most Embarrassing Messy House Story
—The Night Bandit—
BY TOMMY L.

Once when I was in my twenties, I came home from a date to find a surprise in my bedroom. Living on the third floor of an old apartment building in an urban area, I had left the window open without a screen, never expecting a raccoon to climb inside and make himself at home on my desk.

I called the police, who came right away. Not knowing what else to do, they stood in the doorway of the bedroom and threw things at the animal until it finally got fed up and left, climbing out the way it had come in. We then closed the window behind it.

As the cops were leaving, I thanked them for their trouble. They said it was no problem, but that it was a shame I hadn't gotten home before the raccoon tore my whole bedroom apart.

Red-faced, I didn't have the nerve to tell them that the raccoon hadn't done a thing. The bedroom looked like that before the animal got there!

22

A Final Word

The end of a matter is better than its beginning,
and patience is better than pride.

ECCLESIASTES 7:8

When I first began to come up with the House That Cleans Itself System, I didn't have much more than a theory, some determination, and the belief God was leading me in a new and exciting direction. At that time I had no idea what the future would hold for my radical approach to housekeeping, least of all that it would eventually branch beyond the walls of my own home. I just knew I had to do *something* to fix my problem and that the time for listening to the cleaning experts was over.

Because I was starting from scratch with no book or pretested plan to guide me, it took a long time to convert my home into a House That Cleans Itself. But once I was finished, not only had I ended my own lifelong struggle with mess, I also found that by sharing my story with others I was able to help end their struggle as well.

All these years later, we are still living in a House That Cleans Itself. We still use HTCI thinking for every new item we acquire, every rearrangement of furniture, and so on. Even so, we have learned the hard way that the system *can* fall apart once in a while. When that happens, it's always for the same three-fold reason: We acquire new stuff, but we don't get rid of any old stuff, and we don't assign a place for the new stuff.

Given that both my husband and I are pack rats by nature, that's our biggest ongoing challenge. For me, it's not that I have trouble getting rid of things; it's simply that I don't take the time often enough to do so. Whenever we reach that tipping point and the house starts to get out of control again, I know it's time for another big purge. At least with a House That Cleans Itself, it's easy to see what needs correcting and then take the proper steps to fix it.

Over the years the most important lesson I have learned is that a House That Cleans Itself is more of an ongoing mentality than a one-time conversion process. As long as we remember that, the system continues to work like a dream and our house continues to stay clean.

Recently, I had an experience that drove home to me just how far I have come in this area. My husband and I were in the process of refinancing to take advantage of new, lower interest rates when one morning he called me from the office.

"Sorry I forgot to tell you," he said, "but the appraiser will be coming by the house this morning to take a look at everything."

"Everything?"

"Yep. He just has to walk around and see each room, probably take some pictures, make some notes, and then he'll leave."

At that point, the old Mindy—the pre-HTCI Mindy—would have either fainted or had a heart attack or flown into a screaming fit.

No advance warning? Every single room? Photos and everything?

Instead, all I said was, "Thanks a lot for the advance warning, honey. I don't have time right now to run around and straighten up."

"You'll be fine," he replied. "I think we're in pretty good shape."

And later, when the man arrived and I took a break from my writing to walk him from room to room, I realized it was true. Sure, there was a counter that needed wiping down. A toilet that could have used a swishing with a toilet brush. Some papers that had piled up. Recyclables overflowing in one of the bins. Some crumbs on the floor around a chair.

But by and large, I had nothing to be embarrassed about. A total stranger showed up with almost no advance warning and took pictures of every room in my house...*and I was not ashamed*. If that's not the single best endorsement for the effectiveness and transformative power of a House That Cleans Itself, then I don't know what is.

Things around my house really aren't like they used to be. Not at all. Now that you have read this book, that is my prayer for you as well. As you turn your home into a House That Cleans Itself, you'll begin to see lasting and effective change room after room after room. The system works. Let it work for you.

Then take all that extra time and effort you used to devote to wading through clutter and chaos and give it over to God. He has some wonderful, much better uses for your time and resources than shuffling around a bunch of papers, possessions, dirt, dust, and junk.

He loves you so much. He has big plans for your life.

And He's ready to bless you in ways you've never dreamed possible.

My Most Embarrassing Messy House Story
—Microwave Madness—

BY GINGER S.

I once moved aside a borrowed microwave that my husband and I had been using for several months to put in its place one that had been given to us as a Christmas present. In all the confusion, I forgot to clean the inside of the borrowed one, and it was shoved into the garage.

Months later the friend who loaned the microwave to us was at our home for a party. My husband said, "Oh, we can give you back that microwave now." He went to the garage and brought the oven into the party. Before I could react, he popped open the door in front of everyone.

The microwave looked and smelled like something from my worst nightmare. Actually, that whole experience *was* my worst nightmare— except it really happened!

Part 4

Supplemental Content

*My people will live in peaceful
dwelling places, in secure homes,
in undisturbed places of rest.*

Isaiah 32:18

Glossary

ADD/ADHD—attention deficit disorder/attention deficit hyperactive disorder; a chronic neurological behavioral condition common among the housekeeping impaired. ADD can cause difficulties with clutter, organization, time management, and other "executive function" skills.

Barnacling—the tendency to pile stuff on available horizontal surfaces in a home, whether those items belong on those surfaces or not, much as a ship's hull will attract barnacles that latch on and stay.

Camouflage—to decorate or furnish in a way that tends to hide messes such as dirt, pet hair, crumbs, stains, and so forth.

Container limit—the maximum amount one is allowed to accumulate of something within a designated container. Once that amount has been reached or exceeded, action must be taken, such as throwing away the excess or putting it where it belongs.

CONVERT system—a deep-cleaning and organizing system that implements the HTCI principles in each room of a home. The acronym stands for: *Clear out the clutter; Open up and clean; Neaten, organize, and solve problem spots; Verify rabbit trails and set up stations; Examine sight zones; Record future improvements needed*; and *Take steps now for ongoing maintenance.*

Cord clutter—mess created by electronic cords that have been bunched together in an unlabeled and jumbled fashion; commonly found near televisions, computer, small appliances, charging stations, etc.

Deep clean—intense, involved cleaning that a home requires on a regular, periodic basis.

Engineer convenience—make it as easy to be neat as it was to be messy. Find solutions for the root causes of recurring messes and make changes to the house so that the mess-inducing behaviors will no longer cause those messes to happen

Expected messy areas—areas in a home that inevitably become messy on a repeated basis.

First impression of clean—subconsciously deciding that a room is clean at first sight, whether or not the room is completely clean from one end to the other. This impression can be "engineered" by use of the sight zone principle.

Hoarding—the behavior of acquiring too much and discarding too little. Hoarders have a deep-rooted need to keep things. Letting go of stuff creates great anxiety, which causes a vicious cycle of acquiring, clinging, and denial. Hoarders create such clutter-filled living spaces that those spaces cannot be used for their intended purposes.

Home base zone (HBZ)—the one area in a home that, when clean, relieves the stress of the homemaker. This zone varies person to person and can be anything from a dish-free kitchen sink to an orderly, well-made bed.

House That Cleans Itself—a home that has been set up to engineer cleanliness, thus greatly reducing the inhabitants' cleaning time and efforts.

HTCI—acronym for House That Cleans Itself.

Inevitable invisibles—imperfections such as stains, nicks, or frays that contribute to an overall feeling of "unclean" but that have become unnoticeable to the homeowner over time.

Intermediate clean—periodic vacuuming, mopping, and other moderate-level cleaning activities.

Label maker—handheld battery-operated device that prints out labels for use with home organization.

Magic Eraser—a cleaning product that can be used to rub away hard-to-remove stains, scratches, and scuff marks from a variety of surfaces.

Necessary messes—those areas in a home that might appear cluttered to an outsider but are in fact necessary and functional, such as the family bulletin board or the front door launching pad.

Prayer walk—a form of worship that involves praying as one moves from room to room throughout one's home. Prayer walking can focus efforts, reaffirm priorities, and provide the opportunity to ask for God's blessings upon home and family in very specific ways.

Put-Away Style (PAS)—the manner in which one usually puts an item away when finished with it.

Quick clean—cleaning that can be done quickly and easily, whenever one has a moment to spare. For example, wiping out the microwave while waiting for bread to toast.

Rabbit trails—the journeys one takes when searching for the tools required to perform specific tasks such as wrapping a gift, making coffee, or mailing a package. These round-the-house hunts waste energy, time, and patience as well as contribute to mess and clutter.

Sight zone—the area first seen when standing in the doorway of a room and looking inside. (A room with multiple doorways will have multiple sight zones.)

Stations—a collection of items needed for a given task, placed in a single container when possible, and stored in the room where the task is most likely to be performed.

Swiffer WetJet—a bucketless mopping system that dispenses cleaning fluid at the push of a button and then wipes the floor with a disposable cleaning pad.

"Up and Away" principle—decorating and furnishing in such a way that objects are mounted on the wall, which allows for easier, faster cleaning of surfaces.

Having a Yard Sale the HTCI Way

Before you begin sorting

- Decide whether the sale will be done alone or with others.
- Choose a sale date.
- Find out local rules and restrictions and file any necessary paperwork.
- Decide on advertising and write ad(s).
- Decide what will be done with leftover items immediately after sale and make arrangements for that to happen.
- Buy preprinted price stickers and Sharpie markers.
- Gather boxes and trash bags.
- Label one large box "Clean" and one "Repair."
- Prepare a place in or near your home to store each box of items as it is filled.
- Visit a few local yard sales to get an idea of how your items should be priced. Especially note the going rate for one-price-fits-all items such as clothes and books.

As you sort

+ Place the items you'll be selling into boxes or bags.

+ Set aside any items that need to be cleaned or repaired before the sale into the "Clean" and "Repair" boxes, respectively.

+ If you'd like, set aside any Bibles into a box marked "Free." You'd be amazed at how pleased some people are to get a free Bible—and how good it feels to know you spread God's Word that quickly and easily.

+ At the beginning of each sorting session, go through the items you boxed up the day before and put price stickers on them. Note that while this is less efficient than pricing as you sort, for the housekeeping impaired it is far easier and faster in the long run to do it separately. It also gives a nice emotional boost for a new day of purging, because it reminds you that not only are you de-cluttering, but you're also going to earn a little cash in the process. Remember, however, as you set your prices that your ultimate goal here is not to make money—it's to get rid of stuff, so price low.

+ To keep things simple at the cash register, forget nickels, dimes, and pennies. Price everything using the "quarters and dollars" method: Items under a dollar should be rounded to the nearest quarter—25¢, 50¢, or 75¢— while items costing more than that should be rounded to the nearest dollar—$1, $2, $3, $5, $12, $20, etc.

+ For any items so small or junky they are not even worth a quarter, either put them in baggies with other similar items and charge a quarter for the whole thing, or assemble a box of "free with purchase" items that sits next to the cash register. (This has proven very popular at our yard sales, especially with kids. They love to go through and pick out some little free toy while their mom shops.)

✦ On days you don't feel like sorting, focus on cleaning and repairing. Often, a quick run through the dishwasher or washing machine can work wonders on items that seem faded and old. Any items that can't be repaired should be discarded unless you know for a fact they can be sold for parts. Be sure to label those as broken, however.

✦ Set aside plastic grocery bags for the day of the sale.

As the sale gets closer

✦ Make signs.

✦ Get change (bills and coins).

✦ Round up a fanny pack or a locking money box.

✦ Find friends or family willing to help.

✦ Gather tables, refreshments, chairs, trash bags, plastic grocery bags, and an extension cord.

✦ Hang signs.

The day before the sale

✦ Hang more signs/check signs you've already hung to make sure they're still up.

✦ Set up tables where your items will be displayed.

✦ Set up chairs for your workers in the shade, if possible.

✦ Run an extension cord from the house to show the functionality of any electrical devices you'll have for sale, such as lamps or stereos.

✦ Reconfirm arrangements for what will be done with leftover items.

The day of the sale

+ Be aware that people will show up long before you're officially open for business. Try not to let them distract you. Just start early, keep setting up, and sell to them if they find something they want, but don't waste your time before the sale haggling prices or digging through unloaded boxes trying to find the sorts of things they are asking for. Your main goal is to be set up and ready to roll by the time stated in your ad and on your signs, not to please a few intrusive early birds who think it's okay to jump the gun.

+ Remind yourself and your team that the primary goal is to get rid of stuff, not to make money. Let people bargain with you. Offer "super sales" on various items as the day progresses. Occasionally go around with a Sharpie, cross out what's written on the tags, and mark things even lower. Sell, sell, sell!

+ Once the sale is finished, follow through with your "after plan" and don't allow a single leftover item back into your home. Even if your after plan is simply to give away what's left, mark all of it with a big "FREE" sign and put it at the end of the driveway. Then don't look again until it's all gone. You said goodbye to those items the day you first decided they would be in the sale. No second-guessing, no take backs, no regrets.

Now count your cash, treat yourself to an ice-cream cone, and go enjoy the point of it all: your less-cluttered home!

Shopping the HTCI Way

> Whenever shopping for your home, let your motto be:
> ## *"Camouflage and simplicity!"*

Handy HTCI Shopping Tips

+ When buying clothes, consider instituting a "no dry cleaning" rule. Fabric technology has come so far that even the fanciest of evening wear can often be found in hand- or even machine-washable versions.

+ Avoid household systems that require using hooks, such as key racks or earring holders, whenever possible. Use containers instead.

+ Look to the industrial supply world for clever solutions to household problems, such as disposable shoe covers for muddy boots or a sturdy baker's rack for storing unfinished projects.

+ Instead of using a conventional jewelry box, consider clear acrylic divided holders from the organizing section of an office supply store. Place items such as earring pairs in individual sections.

✦ For bedding, choose comforters that hide imperfections. In general, the thicker the comforter, the more forgiving it is of bumpy blankets and sheets underneath. This is especially helpful for smaller children who are just learning to make their beds as well as busy adults who don't have time to do it perfectly every day.

✦ Never buy any bedding, including blankets and comforters, that can't be machine washed.

✦ Never buy any washable item for your home, such as a comforter, that's bigger and thicker than will fit inside your washing machine.

✦ If you habitually do something in a messy fashion, don't buy visible storage for it. For example, that lovely acrylic makeup caddy may look nice atop your dresser, but not if you tend to put your makeup on in a hurry and then leave a jumble of tubes and bottles all over the dresser. Opt for drawer storage instead, so that when you're finished all that's required for cleaning is to scoop the items back into the drawer (as opposed to carefully returning them to their individual slots in a caddy).

✦ If your household plants are allowed to get thirsty too often, they will drop leaves or contribute to a messy feel by always looking droopy or brown. To keep this from happening, make them self-watering. A variety of devices for this are on the market, including self-watering containers (with a reservoir in the bottom and wicking material to slowly draw the water up to the plant), water-retaining crystals, watering balls, and water-absorbing mats. You'll still have to refill them from time to time, but not nearly as often as you do now. Check online for "self-watering plants" or visit a local gardening center for more information.

✦ To prevent bringing even more dirt from the outside in, every home should have two brooms: an exterior one and an interior one. Make sure they look completely different so no one confuses the two.

+ If you use a treadmill in your house, buy a pair of shoes that are specifically and only for that treadmill. Never wear them outside. The shoes will stay cleaner, which in turn will keep the treadmill cleaner. In fact, without sending loose dirt particles along the belt as it passes by, you may even extend the life of the machine.

+ Remember, for the housekeeping impaired, *most organizational products create more mess than they help to contain.* Never purchase any organizational product unless you are buying it to serve a specific function in a predesignated place. Such a purchase should be made only after you have measured for it and determined the exact size, shape, and type of organizer you need. Buying random organizational products because they seem like they may work is a common temptation but a big mistake and one you must try to resist.

+ No House That Cleans Itself is complete without a pack of "furniture markers." These are felt tip markers in shades of browns and blacks, available in hardware and furniture stores, that are designed to hide smaller nicks and scratches in wood.

+ Invest in a label maker to help with sorting and keep your storage areas neat. Label makers are available in a variety of sizes, shapes, and price ranges. Check your local office supply or discount store. Be sure to buy batteries and a few extra rolls of label tape to have on hand as well. Using a label maker is as simple as typing the words you need on a small keyboard, pressing the print button, and watching the label shoot out of the machine.

+ When buying furniture, avoid multiple surfaces as much as possible. (For example, go for all wood or all metal.) Remember, uniformity equals ease in cleaning.

+ When buying furniture, avoid dust-gathering detail work, such as grooves, ornate iron scrolling, and inlays whenever possible.

+ When buying furniture or cabinetry, choose a wood finish that is neither too light nor too dark. Dirt hides best somewhere in the middle.

+ When buying shelves, consider glass-enclosed shelving to prevent dust. Dust will still accumulate on the shelves but much more slowly, turning a weekly dusting chore into one that only needs to be done every few months.

+ When choosing countertops, natural stone such as granite and quartz are the most durable, show the least amount of crumbs and dirt, offer some natural antibacterial properties, and are the easiest to keep clean and looking new. If you prefer a different surface, or your budget doesn't include real stone, there are many other alternatives, each with its own plusses and minuses. Talk to your kitchen designer before you decide.

+ If you're renovating a kitchen or bathroom, consider having your sink and faucet undermounted for ease of cleaning, as that eliminates the "lip." (Also remember that the deeper the kitchen sink, the better it is at hiding dirty dishes.)

+ When you plan to buy laminate or tile flooring, get samples of your favorite designs so you can conduct a House That Cleans Itself experiment first. Bring the samples home and place them on the floor in the dirtiest areas of your house (in front of the sink or just inside the back door). Ignore them for a week. At the end of the week, check all of the samples closely and see which one did the best job hiding the dirt and mess. Let that be your deciding factor for which design you choose.

+ When purchasing large appliances, think fingerprints, fingerprints, fingerprints. Once you've narrowed down your options, do the following test: Place your hand flat against the outside surface, then remove your hand and study the effect from several angles, close and far. Choose the type of finish that hides your handprint best.

+ When buying small appliances, think up and away. Many small appliances come in versions that can be mounted under your cabinets, including toasters, coffeemakers, can openers, televisions, electric toothbrushes, and more.

+ When making larger household purchases—from windows to siding to toilets, be sure to check for the latest in self-cleaning options. Self-cleaning technology is advancing all the time.

As You Shop, Remember...

The fewer surfaces and finishes in your home, the fewer products and processes will be required to keep them clean.

Simple choices equal simple cleaning, so avoid ornate, highly detailed furnishings and other possessions whenever possible.

Every single item you purchase won't just cost you money, it will also now and forever cost you time. Make sure that whatever you're about to purchase isn't just worth the pennies but also the minutes. Life is about more than just stuff!

Item Donations to Organizations

Complete the following table for places such as Goodwill, thrift stores, veterans groups, church yard sales, and more.

Place or organization	Address	Phone #	Pickup or Drop off (circle one)	Days/Dates/ Times	Rules & Restrictions	Needs	Notes	Where stored until pickup
			P D					
			P D					
			P D					
			P D					
			P D					
			P D					

Item Donations to Organizations

Place or organization	Address	Phone #	Pickup or Drop off (circle one)	Days/Dates/ Times	Rules & Restrictions	Needs	Notes	Where stored until pickup
			P D					
			P D					
			P D					
			P D					
			P D					
			P D					

Item Donations to Individuals

Complete the following table for individuals in need, found through churches, homeless shelters, women's shelters, recovery groups, mental health agencies, and other local social service organizations.

Recipient	Reason	Liaison (if any)	Phone # of recipient or liaison	Pickup or delivery arrangements, including day, time, & location	Needs	Does not need	Notes	Where stored until pickup

Item Donations to Individuals

Recipient	Reason	Liaison (if any)	Phone # of recipient or liaison	Pickup or delivery arrangements, including day, time, & location	Needs	Does not need	Notes	Where stored until pickup

Item Sales via Local Outlets

Complete the following table for items you plan to sell via local outlets such as consignment shops, used furniture stores, and used book stores.

Place	Consigner code, if any	Name of contact	Phone #	Address	Times/ dates for drop off	Needs	Rules & Restrictions	Seasonal requirements	Notes

Item Sales Via Internet

Complete the following table for items you plan to sell online, such as through EBay, Craigslist, or amazon.com.

Website	User Name	Password	Account #	Notes

Evidence Record

Location	Evidence	Reason/Root Cause	Solution

Contact Mindy

Want even more info and help with your House That Cleans Itself? Then be sure to check out my blog:

www.thehousethatcleansitself.com

where you'll find all sorts of fascinating tips, articles, photos, how-tos, and more.

Also, be sure to visit my website:

www.mindystarnsclark.com

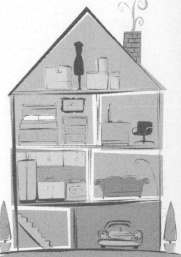

where you can find more tips for your home, download helpful forms, and even read chapter excerpts from this and other books I have written. While you're there, sign up for my e-newsletter and receive your choice of a free HTCI sponge or a 3-pack of e-articles, including:

+ How to Vacuum Just Once a Month,
+ Renovate Your Kitchen the HTCI Way, and
+ Special Encouragement to Mothers with Small Children

If you have an embarrassing messy house story of your own, I'd love to hear it. Send me your story via e-mail to Mindy@mindystarnsclark.com, or via regular mail to Mindy Starns Clark, PO Box 38, Dresher, PA 19025. Unless you ask me not to, I reserve the right to share your tale on my website, blog, and in future books, though of course I will keep your name anonymous. I look forward to hearing from you.

God bless you and your very own House That Cleans Itself!

Notes

Chapter 10—Make It a Team Effort

1. Anna D. Johnson, et al., "Order in the House! Associations Among Household Chaos, the Home Literacy Environment, Maternal Reading Ability, and Children's Early Reading," *Merrill-Palmer Quarterly*, October 1, 2008, http://muse.jhu.edu/login?uri=/journals/merrillpalmer_quarterly/v054/54.4.johnson.pdf.

2. Jackie Fisherman, "Home Smart Home," *Psychology Today*, July 1, 2001, http://www.psychology today.com/articles/200107/home-smart-home.

3. Stephen Goode, "Couples Best Steer Clear of Closet Organizers," *Insight on the News*, May 14, 2001, http://www.questia.com/read/1G1-74440082/couples-best-steer-clear-of-closet-organizers.

4. Daily Mail Reporter, "Couples argue 312 times a year (mostly on Thursday at 8pm for ten minutes)," January 18, 2011, http://www.dailymail.co.uk/femail/article-1348308/Couples-argue-312-year-likely-8pm-10-minutes.html#ixzz1CUVAEmPo.

5. Nissa Hanna, Iconoculture e-newsletter 03/02/2010, http://blog.iconoculture.com/2010/03/02/spring-cleaning/.

6. Goode, "Couples Best Steer Clear of Closet Organizers," *Insight on the News*, May 14, 2001, http://www.questia.com/read/1G1-74440082/couples-best-steer-clear-of-closet-organizers.

Chapter 18—Mind over Matter

1. Tara Parker-Pope, "A Clutter Too Deep for Mere Bins and Shelves," *The New York Times*, January 1, 2008, http://www.nytimes.com/2008/01/01/health/01well.html.

2. "So Much Clutter, So Little Room: Examining the Roots of Hoarding," HealthyPlace.com, January 5, 2009, http://www.healthyplace.com/anxiety-panic/ocd-center/ so-much-clutter-so-little- room- examining- the-roots-of-hoarding.

Chapter 19—Of Marriage and Mess

1. According to Helen Lerner, MD, a physician who works with clutterers and hoarders, those who obsessively cling to sentimental objects usually have a deep-seated fear of scarcity vs. a trust in abundance, a belief that the "good times" can go away and not come back. These types of items serve as an unconscious form of "insurance" against that fear, to protect themselves for when that ultimately happens. (As long as they have their mementoes, the thinking goes, they can survive the lack of good times in the future because at least they will be able to surround themselves with memories of the past.) Dr. Lerner's treatment approach is to explore the emotional genesis of that fear, perhaps tracing back to some point in their life when the good times actually *did* go away, for example, because of a divorce, death, financial reversal, move, or some other major life shift that caused them to experience a great loss. Usually by grieving that loss they are able to work through their pain, overcome that fear, and ultimately reduce their need to hoard substituted sentimental clutter.

To learn more about Harvest House books and
to read sample chapters, log on to our website:

www.harvesthousepublishers.com

HARVEST HOUSE PUBLISHERS
EUGENE, OREGON